A View from Street-Level

The Answer to "Why?"

A.E. LUCAS, JR.

HAVE YOU EVER WONDERED....?

* WHY ARE INCREASING NUMBERS OF YOUNG BLACK MEN IN AMERICA, KILLING EACH OTHER?

* WHY CAN'T THE COMMUNITY, POLICE, COURTS, AND PRISONS, STOP THE VIOLENCE EATING AWAY AT BLACK AMERICA LIKE A CANCER?

* WHY SO MANY BLACK MEN RESPONDED TO THE UNIQUE CALL FOR THE "MILLION-MAN MARCH?"

* WHY RALLIES, PROTESTS, MARCHES, PRAY- INS, AND DEMONSTRATIONS, HAVE NOT ENDED THE SUFFERING OF BLACK PEOPLE IN AMERICA?

* WHY ARE INCREASING NUMBERS OF BLACK MEN GOING INTO THIS NATION'S PRISONS?

THE ANSWERS ARE IN THIS BOOK!!

CONTENTS

CONTENTS *(cont.)*

PROLOGUE

It had been another tough day, and I was tired. As luck would have it, this was my last assignment before the end of my shift. It was a family notification. The kind every police officer dreads. What happened on that night, and the question posed me, impacted me greatly. I had to find the answer. I invite you to join me on a journey through a maze of misconceptions and deceptions, which have plagued a particular group of Americans for one-hundred and forty-eight years. Americans of African descent are this group. We are destroying each other. We mistrust each other. We have no real unity. Why?

No one seems to be able to answer this question. I now offer you a theory and possible 'answer.' One that I learned from the combination of <u>my</u> view of life on the streets as a D.C. Police Officer, as a Marine Corps military policeman, in the court system as a U.S. Marshal, and within the infamous Lorton prison as a Correctional Officer. The issues that I explore deal with 'institutionalization.' This is the end result of long-term *incarceration which 'conditions' a prisoner, to accept his or her form of captivity.*

Africans brought to America were imprisoned, broken, and domesticated like animals. They were conditioned to believe that they were human property. During the hundreds of years of their captivity, a 'generational-institutionalization,' was created. This is a unique form of institutionalization, which affects all African-Americans to this day. From it, a sub-culture has grown and taken root. A sub-culture sprung from a foundation of lies. And like all things built on weak foundations, it eventually collapses. Walk with me on my journey for an answer, and see Black America in a brutally honest view from the 'street-level.'

A VIEW FROM STREET-LEVEL

I have been a sworn law enforcement officer for over four decades. Enough time to see a complete picture of America. It is a nation divided by two realities. One "Black" and the other, "White." In my official capacity, I have served both of these sides of America. Sometimes, to relieve the stress of the job, I thought of other names for the work I performed. One name was "street-doctor." I thought of myself as "on-call," patching-up one problem after another. Never knowing what the next call would be, or how bad.

In a way, police officers are gauges to the health of a community. By the number, and types of calls each responds to, a pattern of the "health" of a community emerges. The majority of my career has been spent in the communities of Black America. I have served on the cold streets, in the city in which I was born. The

Black side of the city is my "patient." I have felt its "pulse." It is in critical condition. From Los Angeles to Washington, D.C., the picture I currently see is grim. Violence and drug abuse are everywhere, and the victims are not only the abusers, but their families and friends as well.

Every day, the media assaults our senses with an over-exaggerated focus on "Black-on Black, and Black-on-White" crime. To maintain our sanity, many of us avoid even looking at it or listening to it. The fear that is generated from this one-sided view is evident. We bar our windows and doors, and alarm our vehicles and homes. We smother our children, to protect them. We watch our neighbors closely, and are wary of strangers. People on the street avoid each other's eyes. Many of us stay off the streets at night, and those that must venture out, are increasingly carrying "something" for their protection.

The police, courts, and prisons, are crowded and over-worked. City hospital emergency rooms on some nights look like war-zones. Shock-Trauma units, on many weekend nights, can run-out of available bed-space. In the schools, the teachers are becoming fearful of their students. Violence in the schools is an ever-increasing phenomenon. Children are killing their siblings, parents, and each other, in shocking numbers. The selling, and use of drugs, has lowered to the elementary school level. Government and private-sector shelters for battered women and the homeless, have started placing armed guards on their doors to prevent escalating violence.

The violent reactions of people turned-away because of lack of space. Local food banks have lines that extend around the corners of their buildings, of people waiting for food to eat. Black churches, always a haven in the community for those in need, find that today there is more need than available resources. As a police officer, I have heard so many anguished cries, from the souls of the citizens I have sworn to protect. I have been a silent witness to the agony and heart-wrenching pain, suffered by Black families who lost a member through violence. On this particular day, it was my duty to notify a mother, that her son had been killed.

He was shot in the head, during a drug-deal gone wrong. The shock of her son's death, made her scream and hold on to me for support. In her grief and anger, her grip tightened on my arms. The strength in her hands, made me wince. Sobbing uncontrollably, she raised her tear-stained face to mine and screamed, "Why? Officer, tell me *please*...why did those Black men DO this? **Why do you Black men KILL each other**? **WHY?** I couldn't answer the poor woman's question. As a police officer, you must respond to *all* types of calls, for assistance. Through experience, you are able to answer almost any question the public might bring to you.

As a senior officer, I took *pride* in my ability to do this. I was well-trained in general and family-crisis intervention. And, I had an advantage in the performance of my duties. This was my city, and these were my people. "To protect and serve" my community, was *personal.* That night, and for the first time in my entire career, I was stumped. I couldn't *answer* this mother's anguished question. "...*Why, do you Black men kill each other?*" The *enormous* array of police assistance available to me at the touch of my radio couldn't help me.

A 'black man' was someone I had *been,* my entire *life.* If anyone *could* have been able to answer the question of "why do you kill each other?" it *should have been me.* Yet I was unable to respond. Most cops wouldn't even try. "Sorry for your loss, ma'am," is the most anyone *could* say. After leaving that house, and for many years *afterwards*, her question haunted me. *Why do* Black men kill each other? Police officers, learn to callous themselves, against much of the public's pain. If you empathize too much, it burns you out. Do your job, and go home to your family. Let the events of the night, drop off of you, when you check-off.

I knew this, but for some reason, _that question bothered me._ After I checked-off, it stayed with me. It tucked itself into the back of my mind, and became that 'small pebble, in my shoe.' An 'irritation,' that began my quest for the truth. I started my search, for the answer to "why?" *Why? Why do* Black men hate and kill each other, disproportionately *more* than *other* races in America? This journey would cause me to *re-*

6

examine, *who* and *what* I was. I was an African *and* an American. That was so easy to *say,* but for most of my life, almost *impossible* for me to *balance. Something* has always been *missing,* from the two. As if an important part of *both* of these halves, was absent.

My quest for an answer would eventually shed light on the missing part of my two halves.

STARTING THE SEARCH FOR THE ANSWER TO WHY?

A good investigator examines all of the facts of a case. Utilizing clues, evidence, eyewitness accounts, and prescribed procedure, he backtracks to a possible motive and suspect. I followed basic police procedure, in my search for the answer to "Why?" The basics are who, what, when, where, how, and why? The first question, is who? This was of course, African-American males. What? We are killing each other for little or no reason. When? We kill in the day or at night. Where? It occurs predominately in our own communities, in black neighborhoods. How? Our weapon of choice is a handgun. Why? My mind can fathom no reason.

I wasn't the only one that was stumped by this particular question. Every cop that is involved in these kids' violent aftermath asks the same question.

Every family notified of an injury or death of a loved one, asks this same question. Black people listening to the news, watching television, or reading the newspaper, have all asked the same question. "Why?" Of course, there is the overt and easy answer. "Young black people are just losing their minds!" But it's much more than that, isn't it?

Their reasons for killing have run the gambit of human emotion. Some want revenge for some real or imagined hurt. There are drug interactions where someone is cheating someone else of their cut or their pay. Or someone tried to rob someone of their money or stash. They even kill someone because they are out of their minds on some chemical. Jealousy, or rage over losing their girlfriend. There is gang-related violence over turf. Or it could be self-defense against a larger aggressor. Envy over some material possession. All of these and more can be laid at their feet.

These seemed to be only excuses. There were just too many deaths, to be easily explained away by these excuses. I needed to know the real truth. I studied the men, watched them, and talked to them extensively. The level of anger, defense, anticipation of any slight, and eagerness to immediately retaliate, led me to an inescapable conclusion. Something was wrong with our perception of reality. There was a tangible element of fear between us. Listening to the men talk, many of them confessed that they "stayed open to any possibility" with each other. Meaning, that a

Black man had to be on-guard around other Black men, at all times.

You never knew what was going to happen. This attitude appeared systemic, and covered all age groups and all parts of our community. It appears in young Black men from the projects, older Black men from middle-class homes, and even seniors, playing checkers in the park. All of these men seem normal, until they become upset. Then, the truth comes out. You see a deep mistrust and hatred for one other. Since it covers all age groups, and crosses all economical and social lines, the reason *has* to lie hidden in areas not thoroughly researched before.

I talked to many different people, to discover some over-lapping causation. All of the people that I talked with gave different reasons for the violence that plagues us. My investigation seemed to be at a stand-still. Meanwhile, the killings increased. Each day, the media seemed to be in a contest, to see which reported crime could "out-shock" the community more. It was during this time, that my law enforcement career changed, again. For over twenty-years, I had been a police officer. In the Superior and U.S. District Courts, I was a Deputy U.S. Marshal. Now, I had decided to become a Correctional Officer, with the D.C. Department of Corrections.

In 1995 they operated the largest, almost entirely all-Black federal prison system, in the United States. The Lorton Reformatory, in Fairfax County Virginia, covered over three-thousand acres of ground. Within this expanse, the District operated seven individual prisons, containing *almost nine-thousand Black men* convicted of misdemeanor and felony offenses. The seven prisons (or "facilities") were, Maximum Security, Medium Security, Minimum Security, Occoquan, Youth Center, Central, and Modular. The two largest prisons, Occoquan (the 'Quack') and Central (the 'Hill'), each contained up to eighteen-hundred Black men.

Both had medium and "medium-high" security inmates, doing soft and hard time. They were unique prisons, in that despite the heinous and oft-times violent nature of many of the convictions, the majority of men resided in open dormitories. Fifty to one-hundred men, many convicted of brutal crimes, sitting on bunks watching the officer watch them. No cells and no walls to separate them. These were one-story dormitories, with more than seventy-five convicts per officer. No other federal prison in America operated like Lorton. Only the 'Maximum' Facility had individual cells for their prisoners.

'Max' was run, like a maximum-security prison should be operated. The only problem was, it had *only six-hundred cells*. For the first time in over two decades of law enforcement, I was faced with the challenge of enforcing the law without a gun. No bulletproof vest, mace, shotgun, nightstick, or readily available back-up. Just my keys, ink pen, radio, and logbook. The mental stress associated with making such a drastic change, was heightened by the fact that I was surrounded by men that *I knew.*

The District of Columbia boasts a population of over six-hundred thousand citizens, but that's a deception. It is not homogenous. For most of my life, Washington, D.C., has been racially *split* down the middle. There were literally, Blacks on one side, Whites on the other. This is similar to *most* southern towns. If you wanted to see the *Black* part of D.C., you would start at Fifteenth Street, N.W, and travel east, to Southern Avenue, S.E. If you wanted to see the *White* part of D.C., you would start at Seventeenth Street, N.W., and travel west to Western Avenue, N.W. The White House, not the U.S. Capitol, was always the silent "racial demarcation line" of the District.

There are almost seventy city blocks across the *Black* side of town, containing around three-hundred thousand people. Some parts of northwest and southwest, and pretty much all of northeast and southeast D.C., are where you found the majority of Black people. Despite the trend of Black folk moving to the suburbs, I have steadfastly remained in the District all of my life. Now, here I was in a prison in Lorton, Virginia, surrounded by almost nine-thousand Black convicts. This is suicide, right? A former police officer unarmed, in the largest all-Black prison in America. Not so. As it turned out, I was predominately surrounded by men *I had grown up with.*

We had played ball, and gone to school together. Many of them I recognized as neighbors and had gone to church with. We knew each other's parents and siblings. Our mothers babysat for each other. Although none of this changed the fact that I was now an officer, I was not viewed as a stranger, or as an enemy. I was just a "home-boy," with a distasteful government job. I did not realize that this place would cause my epiphany, and give me the answer I searched for.

Day after day I watched this enormous group of young and old men, *forced* to live imprisoned together for months and years. It was through *all* of these things, that I would *find* the answer to a heartbreaking question posed to me by a grieving Black mother. *"Why do Black men kill each other?* Working in this unique prison, my learned misconceptions of life in America would dissolve, to expose my *own* "generational-institutionalization."

THE EXCEPTION CLAUSE OF THE THIRTEENTH AMENDMENT

Any good Correctional Officer will tell you, that the key to survival in any prison is good communication skills. *Giving* respect is the way to *gain* respect. That was especially easy for me, because my parents instilled "home-training" and manners in me as a young child. In addition, I like people, and had a lifetime of public service. As a police officer, you either learn to understand people, or the stress of dealing with them will burn you out. I consider myself the "luckiest" guy in law enforcement. I have worn the badges of the *entire* criminal justice system in Washington, D.C. As I like to say, "I have worked the system from lock-up, to let go."

It's a wonderful thing, not to be bored with your job. And believe me, surrounded by eighteen-hundred convicts it's *impossible* to be bored. Something is always going on. With so many people "doing time," the clock rules your life. The daily routines become mechanical. Sitting at my dormitory desk, making log entries, the men talk to you in passing. The officer's desk is situated next to the entrance door, to observe everyone who enters or leaves. Any and all types of conversations are struck, all around an officer. On this one particular day, I was listening to an intriguing argument between two 'old timers,' and a young 'first-timer.'

They were admonishing him against using the word "nigger," when he spoke to them. They were explaining to him, for a Black man to use the "N" word was self-degrading. To which he replied, "What you want me to call myself, a *"slave"*?" One of the older men shot back at him, "read the Thirteenth Amendment to the Constitution, *convict*, and you'll see that's **exactly** what you are!" An argument ensued, and I had to break them up. I must confess though, that I was intrigued. Their conversation left me curious as to what the older man was referring to, when he said "read the Thirteenth Amendment....you'll see that's *exactly* what you are."

This is the Nation's Capital. I knew *exactly* where to go, to have a look at this famous document. On my day-off, I went to the National Archives Museum, the 'home' of the United States Constitution. For fifty-cents, I purchased a copy of "The United States Constitution, and fascinating facts about it." It promised to be interesting, so I started reading.

Amendment XIII.

The Thirteenth Amendment was ratified December 6, 1865.

Section 1. *"Neither slavery nor involuntary servitude, except as a punishment for crime whereof the party shall have been duly convicted, shall exist within the United States, or any place subject to their jurisdiction."*

I inquired if there were *more content* to this Amendment, than what I was reading? I was told that the Thirteenth Amendment, was almost *word for word*, the *last* section of the *earlier*

"District of Columbia Emancipation Act." Legislation *also* approved by the Congress, on April 16, 1862. *Three-years before*, the Thirteenth Amendment was ratified. A copy of it can *also* be purchased, at the U.S. National Archives and Records Administration. It *clarifies* the *intent and wording*, of the *later* enacted Thirteenth Amendment.

"An Act for the Release of certain Persons held to Service or Labor in the District of Columbia *Be it enacted by the Senate and House of Representatives of the United States of America in Congress assembled.* **That all persons held to service or labor within the District of Columbia** *by reason of African descent* **are** *hereby discharged and freed of and from all claim to such service or labor;* **and** *from and after the passage of this act neither slavery nor involuntary* *servitude, except for crime, whereof the party shall be duly convicted, shall exist in said District..."* (Emphasis added).

I was stunned. All of my life, I had been taught that "slavery" was *ended* in the United States of America. That President Abraham Lincoln had given slaves their *freedom* by the "Emancipation Proclamation" of 1863, and that the Congress had forever *abolished* slavery by the enactment of the "Thirteenth Amendment" in 1865. Yet, what I was reading meant that slavery *had only been <u>suspended</u>,* by the Congressional legislation approved in 1862, and then "upon conviction," *would resume again!* But a *'slave'* has a *'Master,'* right?

Since the *federal government made this provision,* it means that *'ownership'* of the slave then <u>transfers</u> to the *authority of the United States Government* after any criminal *conviction* of *that Negro!* The institution of slavery went from *<u>private</u>* to *<u>federal government</u>* control. The 1862 Act *applied to Blacks in the District of Columbia.* The Congress had *bequeathed* this authority, to the *very criminal justice system* to which I had devoted my entire adult life. The only differences between the two Congressional actions were that the District Act *specified its intent was for the Negro,* and the *later* enacted Amendment *excluded <u>mention</u>* of the Negro *specifically.*

'Slave' status would now be a *<u>punishment</u> for conviction of a crime. That's* what the old man was referring to, when he told the young man that calling himself a 'slave' was appropriate. He had been 'convicted,' *and* he *was* of *'African descent.'* Therefore, his *punishment* was *that he was now a 'slave.'* It was *impossible* for *anyone* living in 1862, Black or White, to <u>mis</u>understand what a 'slave' was. A 'slave' was "Negro property, bought and bound into servitude for *life*, and *owned* by his master." As <u>*Black*</u> people were the slaves being "freed," *why* would the government *free* them, just to open a <u>*new and future door*</u> that would allow their *'enslavement'* <u>*again*</u>?

I was confused. None of this, made any sense. I always walk whenever something is bothering me, so I started walking down Constitution Avenue. Museums and big trees line the boulevard. It has a calming effect. I sat on a bench, and thought deeply about what I had just read. When slavery was a *publicly-owned business* in North America, slave *owners* dealt with runaways, in *three steps*. First, the 'slave-catchers' were dispatched, to *capture* and *return* the errant slave. Next, the 'Overseer' *punished* the slave, many times brutally, as the *owner* wished. Finally, *after* the slave was punished, he was chained and put on *display* as a *warning* to the other slaves. The Congress of the United States had lied. It never *abolished* slavery. After its suspension and transfer, 'slavery' was made a *judicial* <u>*threat, and put under* <u>*government*</u> *control.*</u> Once *'punished'* with *slavery,* an African was a slave *for life. I* had unwittingly become the *instrument* of the government that *enforced* this law. There are *three* parts to the criminal justice system, as there were three parts to the *slave* system. There are the police, the courts, and the prisons. Is it coincidental that the *police* had become the new 'slave-catchers' after Emancipation?

Police would *'track-down'* the runaway Negro, and take him *back* to the "plantation" courts. The *courts* had become the 'Overseers.' They would 'punish' the former slave, by placing him *back* into *'slavery.'* The *prisons* were where the punished *'slaves'* would be taken for *display,* as a *warning* to the other 'slaves.' As with the original plantation scenario, the *Overseer (the judges),* are in charge of the trackers *and* of doling out the punishment. *Today's* police and corrections are *guided* in *their* duties, by the orders of the *courts.* The courts are *'advised'* in *their* punishment of the 'slave,' by *recommendations from Federal sentencing 'guidelines.'*

Guidelines from the 'slaves' new 'Master' since 1862, the United States Government. The institution of 'slavery' had gone from *overt* (private control) to *covert* (government control), *without* Black people *recognizing* the *subterfuge!* I visited the Library of Congress, the world's greatest repository of historical facts. I was looking for answers, based on my knowledge of the criminal justice system. Take for example, the area of 'parole.' Being an *'enforcer,'* I know that 'parole' was created, to *monitor* and *control the freedom of freed prisoners.*

Any failure on the part of the parolee, to adhere to the *conditions* of release from prison, could cause the government to *revoke* that convict's freedom. The *fear* of criminal recidivism is what keeps the government *monitoring* the convict. This *exception* to the Thirteenth Amendment *now made sense to me. Apparently,* the government was *fearful* of what Blacks *might* do, once *released* into their 'civilized' society <u>*unchecked*</u>. So, it created a means to'*re*-enslave' Black people, as a *control*-mechanism.

This is the way the majority of Americans *believe* that the Amendment is written. **"*Neither slavery nor involuntary servitude shall exist within the United States, or any place subject to its jurisdiction.*"** The passage, read *this* way, <u>abolishes</u> slavery. However, if you now add the *exception,* you can understand how *I* interpreted it. **"*Except* as a punishment for crime where the party shall have been duly convicted,"..** This Amendment *freed* the Negro from *being* a slave *then* warned him that he would *be* a slave <u>*again,*</u> if he *was convicted of a crime.*

As Negroes had just *been* slaves *immediately* <u>*before*</u> ratification of this Amendment, any *violation* of the law leading to *conviction,* would place them <u>*back*</u> into the institution America *had* <u>*just released them from!* </u>*White* people, did not *'own'* <u>*other*</u> *White people.* They 'worked-off' *debts* to each other. They were *apprenticed,* to each other. They were "indentured" to each other. The laws and morals of those times, allowed *only non-Whites, to be 'slaves.'* Therefore, as was apparent by the *clearly truthful* "<u>District of Columbia Emancipation Act</u>" of 1862, *this "exception"* <u>*only*</u> applied to *African* descendants <u>*and*</u> their <u>*future*</u> generations.

So, what I had been told about the "<u>Thirteenth Amendment</u>," had been wrong. It *did not* unconditionally free Black people from slavery. I clearly understood what I read, and there was no mistake. But if *that* was a lie, what about President Abraham Lincoln's famous "<u>Emancipation Proclamation</u>?" This is the document that 'emancipated the slaves,' in 1863. Surely *that* important document was truthful, and actually freed my people from the hell of slavery.

THE DECEPTION OF THE EMANCIPATION PROCLAMATION

I went to the section of the Library of Congress that held the information that I needed, and began to read. Time went by swiftly. When I had finished reading this historical document, I was even more perplexed than before. *Nothing* I had read, *really 'freed' anyone!* It was just designed to make people *believe* that 'slavery' was ended for Black people. Here, is the "Emancipation Proclamation," of January 1, 1863.

By the President of the United States of America: A Proclamation.

Whereas, on the twenty-second day of September, in the year of our Lord one thousand eight hundred and sixty-two, a proclamation was issued by the President of the United States, containing, among other things, the following, to

wit:

"That on the first day of January, in the year of our Lord one thousand eight hundred and sixty-three, all persons held as slaves within any State or designated part of a State, *the people whereof shall then be in rebellion against the United States, shall be then, thenceforward, and forever free;* and the Executive Government of the United States, including the military and naval authority thereof, will recognize and maintain the freedom of such persons, and will do no act or acts to repress such persons, or any of them, in any efforts they may make for their actual freedom.

That the Executive will, on the first day of January aforesaid, by proclamation, designate the States and parts of States, if any, *in which the people thereof, respectively, shall then be in rebellion against the United States;* and the fact that any State, or the people thereof, shall on that day be, in good faith, represented in the Congress of the United States by members chosen thereto at elections wherein a majority of the qualified voters of such State shall have participated, shall, in the absence of strong countervailing testimony, be deemed conclusive evidence that such State, and the people thereof, are not then in rebellion against the United States.

Now therefore I, Abraham Lincoln, President of

the United States, by virtue of the power in me vested as Commander-in-Chief, of the Army and Navy of the United States in time of actual armed rebellion against the authority and government of the United States, *and as a fit and necessary war measure for suppressing said rebellion, do, on this first day of January, in the year of our Lord one thousand eight-hundred and sixty three,* and in accordance with my purpose so to do publicly *proclaimed for the full period of one hundred days, from the day first above mentioned,* order and designate as the States and parts of States wherein the people thereof respectively, are this day in rebellion against the Unites States, the following, to wit: Arkansas, Texas, Louisiana, (except the Parishes of St. Bernard, Plaquemines, Jefferson, St. John, St. Charles, St. James Ascension, Assumption, Terrebonne, Lafourche, St. Mary, St. Martin, and Orleans, including the city of New Orleans) Mississippi, Alabama, Florida, Georgia, South Carolina, North Carolina, and Virginia, (except the forty-eight counties designated as West Virginia, and also the counties of Berkley, Accomac, Northampton, Elizabeth City, York, Princess Ann, and Norfolk, including the cities of Norfolk and Portsmouth[)], *and which excepted parts, are for the present, left precisely as if this proclamation were not issued.*

And, by virtue of the power, *and for the purpose aforesaid,* I do order and declare that all persons held as slaves within said designated States, and parts of States, are, and henceforward shall be free; and that the Executive government of the United States, including the military and naval authorities thereof, will recognize and maintain the freedom of said persons.

And I hereby enjoin upon the people so declared to be free to abstain from all violence, unless in necessary self-defence; and I recommend to them that, in all cases when allowed, they labor faithfully for reasonable wages.

And I further declare and make known, *that such persons of suitable condition, will be received into the armed services of the United States to garrison forts, positions, stations, and other places, and to man vessels of all sorts in said service.*

And upon this act, *sincerely believed to be an act of justice, warranted by the Constitution, upon military necessity,* I invoke the considerate judgment of mankind, and the gracious favor of Almighty God.

In witness whereof, I have hereunto set my hand and caused the seal of the United States to be affixed.

Done at the City of Washington, this first day of January, in the year of our Lord one thousand

eight-hundred and sixty three, and of the Independence of the United States of America the eighty-seventh.

By the President: ABRAHAM LINCOLN WILLIAM H. SEWARD, Secretary of State.

The "Emancipation Proclamation," was *mis-*interpreted. *It only freed slaves who were <u>in the states</u> at war with the Union.* What means did they have to "free" themselves? It was just a ploy. Why? It is a time of great unrest in the nation. We are at war, with each other. The "War Between the States," known as the American Civil War. President Abraham Lincoln had to make a difficult decision. The North had greatly underestimated the South's strength. The South's prolonged determination to preserve its way of life had resulted in severely damaging the North's resources.

The decision to enlist the aid of the Negro, in the battle to re-claim the South to the Union, brought an estimated 180,000 Black troops to the Union Army. They fought valiantly for their own freedom, as well as for the freedom of all Black people in slavery. Despite the small numbers of Blacks who fought on the side of the Confederacy, the enormous numbers of Blacks who enlisted on the side of the Union Army undoubtedly turned the tide in favor of the North. It is my belief that President Lincoln never intended originally, to free the slaves.

From reading his personal papers, I saw where events had "snow-balled," into causing all slaves to *have* to be freed by the United States. The South was winning the War. Lincoln was desperate, and so many freeborn Blacks and runaway slaves, were screaming for a chance to fight for the Union. For them, this war became a way to punish slave owners, and free their people. For President Lincoln, and his generals in the Army, it was an easy way to get massive numbers of fresh troops in their desperate battle to save their union.

So, the 'colored' troops were enlisted and formed. As the War progressed, and the Union Army forged into the Southern states, more and more Blacks swelled the ranks of the Union Army. The aim of the Union Army was *not* to fight for the freedom of Black slaves, but the routing of the Confederacy. It was just a natural by-product of the pandemonium caused by the War, that slaves no longer held under suppression, would flee their master's lands. Those able to could then join with their former master's enemies.

It was at this time, that a simple act of subterfuge on Lincoln's part has been historically *mis*-interpreted by Americans for the past one-hundred and forty-nine years. The "Emancipation Proclamation." In truth, this deceptive document did <u>not</u> 'emancipate' <u>anyone</u>. It was a clever ruse on the part of a desperate North, to cause confusion and misdirection in the ranks of the Confederacy. You see, if you read the "Emancipation Proclamation" carefully, you will note that Lincoln only freed slaves *in Southern states still in rebellion with the Union*. It did *not* free slaves in the *Northern* states, or places in the South already taken-*over* by the Union Army.   Think about this. What good would it do, to 'emancipate' slaves in places you had *no control over?* The Confederacy had its *own* President, and government. It did not *honor* the former government, *or* President. So, *what earthly good would come of Lincoln "freeing" slaves he had no control over?* In truth, he only *did it to create chaos* as a brilliant military tactic. Yet, this man is held in the highest esteem by Black *and* White people today, for *creating* this mis-interpretation. *As a military tactic*, what good would come from "emancipating" these slaves?

How can you expect a slave-owner to concentrate on the war, when the enemy has just told his slaves, that they are *free?* There were no telephones in that day. His mind is on his home, and the question of whether or not his 'slaves' have *run away.* They were intrinsically tied to his wealth. It was clever, but the plan *back-fired* on the Union.   Once having set the stage for these Southern slaves to be freed, there was no *re-enslaving* them. They became a *nuisance* to the Union Armies marching through the South, as their numbers swelled.

There could be no refuge for them, amongst the racist population surrounding them, so many of them followed the only food and protection available. The 'boys in blue' who had 'freed' them. By the Civil

War's end, there were *millions* of freed slaves. What was the government going to do with these millions of freed Blacks? Ending slavery, was *not* the *cause* of the war, it was only a *by-product*. The government's *major* concern at the *end* of the war was the *reason* for the Civil War in the first place.

The South had *seceded* from the Union, because its *wealth* had made it arrogant. It *refused* calls of more taxation. The North envied the South's riches. The wealth that was *created* by slave labor. Once the Civil War was *won,* the United States Government *probably* thought, "what would happen if we give the Southern states *back* their slaves?" The answer was obvious. The South would "rise again." If *you* were in the Congress of the United States at that time, what would *you* do, to keep the southern states from using *slave* labor to quickly become a threat again? Free all the slaves? This would *forever* stop the South from rebellion again.

It was a decision that I believe was ill-planned, and *not* heartfelt. Remember, Washington, D.C., is a *Southern* town. Throughout the long years that slavery flourished, *many Blacks were auctioned into slavery from right here!* That is proof that *pro*-slavery sentiments were alive and well in the Nation's Capital. The abolishment of slavery may have *become* a reality, but I am *certain* that it was no act of *benevolence* on the part of the North. The North desperately needed Negro manpower for the war, *then* used "emancipation" to destroy the enemy. Without slave labor, the south could never regain the wealth needed to 'rise again.'

By satisfying a mild curiosity, I was unraveling many lies, about *my* constitutional freedoms and rights. Things that I had been *taught to believe,* were not so. Two *very* important parts of my structured identity had suddenly, come apart. That I was 'free,' and that 'slavery,' was abolished. What *else* had I been taught, was a 'misconception?' I had inadvertently discovered 'traps' laid for these 'ex-slaves,' *and* their descendants. Lincoln 'freed' slaves in states he *had* no *control* over, but *kept* slavery, in the states that he *did.* The District of Columbia didn't matter, as it *was not then or now,* a "state."

What was the government of the United States so afraid of that would make it *guarantee* its safety, by setting such a severe *penalty* over the heads of <u>every</u> free Negro?   "Slavery shall not exist, **except** as punishment for a crime where the person is convicted." White people could not be made 'slaves,' *only 'indentured servants'* under their laws, *so the punishment of* **'slavery'** *was meant for Black people.* The Library of Congress gave me the *information* I needed, but my past police experience as a Deputy United States Marshal, *answered* my *question of the "release guarantee."* After all, I *worked* for the *new* "master" of my captive race.

WE THE PEOPLE OF THE UNITED STATES...

There are differing opinions from that time frame, on the actual numbers of slaves that were freed. Some say three-million, others say five-million. The *certain* fact was there were *millions* of Black people in bondage in America by 1865. There was something about their release as a massive group that bothered me. Having served as a Deputy United States Marshal, I was trained to *enforce federal and constitutional laws*, under the United States Code. I suddenly realized that America's social contract, its "constitution," was the *key* to the puzzle.

I started to involuntarily laugh as it dawned on me, what the United States Government was *so* afraid of! Quite suddenly, it had several _million_ *free Black-skinned people, right in its midst.* Many of them forever marked by over three-hundred-plus years of cruelty they had suffered at the hands of White-skinned people. *Millions of potential enemies* of the United States of America living side-by-side <u>*with*</u> them, but not <u>*citizens*</u> of the United States at all! Events had happened so fast. Everyone's attention had been on this tragic war, and the numbers killed by it.

The Civil War had finally ended, and Reconstruction had begun. The economy was in a shambles, and the entire *nation's* resources were depleted. Slowly, White people recognized the enormity of what had occurred. These *millions* of Black people in their midst were *not citizens*! They had been *excluded* from the constitutional laws of this country from its inception. And not being "citizens, there was no way to "control" them *unless they broke the law*. Controlling this massive group's "parole," became necessary for America's survival.

Let's look at the times to understand the *terror* this uncontrolled "freedom" of so many Black people, caused White America. It had another "fire" burning that could be "fanned" by the freedom of five million Blacks. The Native-American tribes were starting to *band together* to fight the "White Eyes." The United States government had no idea how many "non-taxed Indians" lived within its borders. There may have been millions of them then. In 1865, the United States was in constant bloody conflict with many of these indigenous tribes of people, and knew them to be intelligent and merciless fighters.

America could *not* ignore the fact that *many*

freeborn Blacks and runaway slaves, had integrated *into* the Indian Nations. Many Native-Americans had also adopted Blacks into their tribes. A large percentage of African-Americans today, are proud of their mixed Native-American and African ancestry. I know that I have Crow blood, from my mother's side of my family tree, which probably accounts for my light-skin and Asian features. I remember my great-grandmother, and the stories of her tribal life.

If *my* example was the 'rule' rather than the 'exception,' then clearly the **early** Native-Americans had no racial prejudice towards the Negro. Their culture, unlike the European, probably accepted the differences between our skin colors. To them, White-skinned men were the same as Black-skinned men. Someone in the government *had* to wonder what would happen if *millions of now-free Blacks* **not covered by the Constitution**, *joined with the Natives* to **<u>fight together</u>** *against their common enemy?* What chance, would a war-weakened North and South have against a combined force of this size?

Didn't the Negro know *every weakness* of his former master? Know all of his secrets? After all, he had been his *property*, for over three-hundred years. By 1868, the American government must have been in a state of *sheer panic*. The first consideration "on the plate" in 1865 however, was the issue of keeping 'control' over these now-freed Blacks. For that, I believe the United States created the Thirteenth

Amendment, and stealthily inserted it's "exception" clause. After all, the exception *does not state whether the 'party' had to commit a 'felony,' or a 'misdemeanor' to be punished with slavery, <u>again</u>.*

It simply states *"whereof the party shall have been duly convicted."* The Congress probably thought that the *threat* of this happening would be enough to keep Black people in line. Three-years *later,* I believe the fear that Blacks *might* join with the Native-American tribes, is what *prompted* the United States to enact *the Fourteenth Amendment.* It was enacted on July 9, 1868 and states that, "All persons born or naturalized in the United States and subject to the jurisdiction thereof, are *citizens* of the United States..." Why would America *free* the slaves then *later,* make them *citizens* of the United States?

Why? *Citizens,* can be *charged with <u>treason</u>, if they <u>consciously</u> or <u>purposely</u> wage war against their own country, or <u>aid</u> its <u>enemies</u>!* In 1865, these now-freed Blacks *were not <u>citizens</u>.* They could go anywhere, and join any nation of people in the world. As I pondered the thought of this strange set of circumstances, another element of America's unique "institutionalization" of Black people came to mind. The 1857 U.S. Supreme Court's ruling of *Dred Scott v. Sanford.* What was the *status* of these millions of slaves, *who were freed* in 1865, *until* they were made *citizens* in 1868?

According to Chief Justice Roger B. Taney in his ruling in March of 1857, *all* Black people in the colonies (free or slave) were *omitted* from the rights of citizenship, *when the constitution was ratified on June 21, 1788. Black-skinned* men, were *not equal or men,* in the eyes of the government. This lunacy continued *past* 1788, and was considered corrected by the 13th Amendment in 1865. Yet there *is no* record of *any* Amendment, legally *restoring that which was taken from them by law for hundreds* of years. Their *equal status as men and women.*

That meant, that this government 'paroled' *non-humans,* who were for all intents and purposes *non-citizens.* Then, three-years later, made these 'non-humans' *citizens!* I believe making 'ex-chattel' citizens under the law, was *also* a control measure. The maximum penalty for treason *is death*, and is enforceable *only* if you *are* a 'citizen.' If free Black 'citizens' tried to join the Native-American tribes to wage war against America, White people would have justification for killing as many Black people as they could!

Although my mind was battered by all of these incredible thoughts assaulting it, one question remained. Why weren't all of these controls done *at the same time?* What caused America in panic, to take *three-years* to place them under its constitution? Of course! I believe it was because *no one in the North* saw the *true* picture of how *many* 'slaves' the South had, *until they were all freed!* Then, as many slowly made their way North they began to see the true picture of their numbers, *and fear gave way to panic.* How *would* they know? 'Slaves,' were by law, *chattel. And chattel was a*

White man's __personal__ property!

Did America know, in 1865, how many *cows* it had in this country? Only *farmers knew.* The *majority* of Americans were *not* slave-*owners.* If they *had* been, the Civil War *would never have started in the first place.* By releasing these *millions* of Black people, the government gave White America one __hell__ of a shock! They had never *seen* such numbers of Black-skinned people, 'free' before. What, of the *slave's* mentality? How, did *they* feel, being *free* for the *first* time in their lives? Free, yet forever *marked* by the color of their skins. Just as 'parolees' are forever marked, by their criminal records.

Unlike parolees, however, these people could be __visually__ *identified.* I needed to know, *how they felt about each other. It is easy to understand that in 1865, few* of these released slaves *even __knew__ each other.* The conditions of their captivity intentionally *separated them.* How *would* they '__know__' one another, other than as fellow "slaves?" I realized the truth. They were *not 'one __people__,' they were one 'group' of people, all freed from imprisonment together!* A massive group of prisoners, who had *nothing* in common with each other except for the mutual color of their skins, who had shared a mutual oppression. *Just like these Black men in the Lorton Reformatory!*

I worked in a unique prison, *with the largest group of Black prisoners anywhere in North America!* Inside this highly unusual open-dormitory and prison-camp setting, *I was a witness to what life must have been like on a Southern plantation!* This Virginia prison was a *massive* industrial work complex, encompassing over 3,000 acres. The prisoners manufactured license plates for the District and federal government vehicles, operated a dairy farm, made clothing, and even had a butcher shop! It operated its own farm, and produced most of its own food. Work-detail inmates were guarded by officers with rifles and shotguns, while they worked the fields.

Suddenly, I was transported back to a time *before* 'emancipation.' *Here* were thousands of Black men, *forced* to live together under a mutual oppression, who had nothing in common except the color of their skins! The two pictures of plantation-prison life, past and present, merged. This is where it all started in America. Here, was an opportunity for me to find the *reasons* Black men *hate each other enough to kill each other*. I needed to study the only group of Black men in America today, who live lives resembling those from our distant past. Here was my chance to find out the truth. The beginning of the "answer to why," *was right in front of me*.

WHAT MADE BLACK AMERICA?

I had to go to the very beginning. The beginning of my ancestor's "slave" past in America. I needed to examine the history of their captivity, and survival, in America. There had to be reasons buried in their past, for the problems surrounding their descendants today. The "beginning" for the majority of "African-Americans," was in the very beginnings of America itself. Although there are isolated references made to Black explorers and 'freeborn' Blacks, the most common denominator that brought the vast majority of Black people to America, was the institution of 'slavery.'

'Slaves' were imported to the continent of America, by earliest accounts, around 1503. This was the period when King Charles I of Spain, first permitted African 'slavery' in his colonies. This practice was then adopted by other Europeans, and legally ended here in 1808, when the United States banned the importation of new 'slaves.' Many nations of Africa, primarily along its western coastline were raided. Hundreds of tribes and many nations were affected by these raids. Millions of Africans were taken by force from their homelands. This was facilitated, by African tribes *selling their captured enemies to Arab and European slavers.*

'Slavery' flourished initially, because of America's need for cheap labor. Later, as farming became more profitable, great farm industries were born. Various physical conditions also played a hand in Europeans choosing Africans for their 'slave' labor. Their ability to work long hours in the hot sun, as well as their inability to 'blend' with the growing European population, made them desirable. The South, being warmer than the North, was perfect for farming. This was one of the reasons why the majority of 'slaves,' were owned by Southern Whites.

Their farming culture, different from the industries of the colder North dictated their need for massive numbers of laborers. Their close proximity to the Spanish Territories, and the shipping routes from the West Indies also made the South the largest depot for the importation of 'slaves.' Finally, the very greed that *created* America's system of 'slavery,' ultimately became its *emancipator.* The South, states below the "Mason-Dixon" line, had climate conditions ideal for year-round planting. Theirs was a massive agrarian culture. The North, on the other hand, depended upon its industrial culture, for its survival.

The Southern States, with such an enormous benefit to their agricultural production from 'slave' labor, saw much more profit than the North. It was *this* disparity, which led to the rift. The call came from the Northern states, for the South to pay more taxes, because of its use of 'slave' labor. The South protested. If the North wanted more money, place it's *free* Blacks into 'slavery.' This issue evoked angry and violent confrontations between the representatives of Northern and Southern States, on the floors of the Congress and Senate.

The South had enough. Southern states' leaders, called for an independent government, separate from the Union. The "War between the States" followed. The end of the Civil War, and the enactments of the Thirteenth, Fourteenth, and Fifteenth Amendments to the Constitution, promised a new beginning for all Black Americans. Or did it? "Jim Crow" laws pushed that promise *aside* for another *century*. The *one-hundred years* that it *finally* took for the government of the United States to *enforce* the laws guaranteeing Black people their rights of citizenship, have left bloody foot-prints on the floor of American history.

They mark a trail of violence and hatred left by American White supremacists. Presidents, members of the Congress and Senate, as well as Supreme Court Justices, denied Black people full integration into White American society. This refusal of the majority of White Americans, to integrate all aspects of their society with Black people, resulted in the gradual emergence of *two* separate societies. Both were rich in the diversities of its people, and *both* were distinctly *different* from one another. One was White. The other, was Black.

AT FIRST I WAS BLIND, BUT NOW I SEE

I am back at work at Lorton. These days, I find myself carrying my notes everywhere. Lorton Prison, as I explained earlier, was a *District* prison in Virginia. It was predominately Black. Seven to nine-thousand Black convicts, all jammed together in a tight complex of seven prisons. You just had to see it, to believe it. On Central Facility, or the "Hill," there were twenty-five dormitories plus modular housing that contained the roughly eighteen-hundred men. During recreation periods, or "rec-time," most convicts would mull around the central courtyard.

The dorm officers kept a dual eye-out for trouble in the yard, as well as in the housing. It was an excellent opportunity for me to observe the prisoners' behavior. Often without being seen myself. Minus their women and children, and all of the material things that made life softer on the outside, their

45

behavior *inside* of the prison was *the same as it was on the outside of the prison!* Only the minority of persons who were born into an educated, and cushioned life *away* from the harsh realities of *ghetto* life, reacted differently to *prison* life.

The *majority* of convicted Black men that I had an opportunity to observe on a daily basis *had* experienced a hard life on the streets. They resembled predators and prey. So *many* of them jammed together and almost *all* of them *strangers* to each other. Despite their common Black skin, *I knew* the truth, *because I knew them*. They were *all* different people, from the same city, in the same prison. That was all. *That* was why they were always on the *defensive,* against each other. Would you expect them to be a *family,* simply because they *all* had *Black* skin?

In prison, the propensity for violence from other convicts, keeps each man aware of his and other's actions around him at all times. Hygiene is maintained, common courtesy and manners are strictly adhered to, and a person's property is respected. Violations of these basic codes could and oft-times *would,* draw *swift and immediate confrontation* with other convicts. Some idea was brushing against my consciousness, but I was enthralled by this man-made reality. Lorton's prisoners live within three concentric social circles.

The outer circle represents the walls of the prison. The next inside circle, are the officers, and their institutional rules. We maintain an authoritative and uniformed hierarchy. The innermost circle, are the convicts. They *also* maintain an established hierarchy that governs the other convicts, contained within the body of space towards the center. Imagine, as I did within Central, that each circle maintains a level of vigilance going *inward* towards the center. And only the *last circle inside, is vigilant in both directions! This* is a prison environment. This was *their* world.

The behavior and attitude amongst the 'group,' is *different,* when the "authority" is not watching them closely. *They revert to predator, and prey. Many* factors play a part in convict hierarchy. Age, physical strength, intelligence, cunning, gangs, convicts who have a 'hook' (can get things done for you, or supply you with 'things'), and convicts who are *known* both inside and out as 'dangerous.' These constantly changing factors dictate who is predator and prey inside of a penitentiary. Watching these imprisoned men, I realized something I had not thought of before.

In the ghettoes of America, *beyond* the sight of the police and courts, *the behavior* of all of these men is *the same.* Having *come* from the *same* neighborhoods that *these* men had come from, I saw the truth. It was at *that* moment, when my epiphany occurred. Standing in the middle of that concrete and asphalt yard, I suddenly saw *two* pictures of *two groups,* blend into *one.* A reflection of the past, melded into the picture I had of the present. A mass of Black *prisoners* became a mass of Black *'slaves!'* What was astonishingly similar was that *both* groups were comprised of African men, whose *perception of reality was altered.*

The past 'slaves' were in reality *prisoners,* who were *taught* <u>by law</u>, that they were 'owned.' Today's 'prisoners,' are in reality *slaves,* who are <u>not</u> *taught* <u>by law</u>, that they are 'owned.' Since the government is the will of the people, and the dominant culture is White, nothing really changed. Only the *ownership papers* did. Even though so much time had passed, both pictures of Africans in my mind's eye were of the same men. *And, they shared the same conditions of living. Although <u>forced</u> together into a shared imprisonment, <u>neither group</u>, were 'one <u>people</u>.'*

One group of *strangers* here, and one group of *strangers* there, separated by one-hundred and twenty-nine years. The truth *blended together.* I swear to you, right there in the yard surrounded by at *least* eight-hundred Black convicts, I started to laugh uncontrollably! The year was 1994, and everyone was staring at me like I was crazy. Maybe I was. It was just an idea, but one that I would start working on that same day. I started asking every 'convict' that I knew one question. They all answered predictably. Later, when I went home, I asked the guys I knew on the street, a *different* question.

Although given different questions, *their* answers were almost *identical* to the answers I had received from the men on the *inside* of the *prison.* The *blended-picture* started to gel in my head. In *both* their mentalities, a *fact* was obliterated, and the memory obscured. What questions did I ask them? On the inside I asked "is a prisoner *owned* by the government?" On the outside I asked "can the government *own* slaves?" The answers I received, both inside the prison and outside the prison, were the same for both groups! They would all respond "no."

Neither group realized that a 'slave,' was an African *prisoner* legally made *"chattel" by the government of the Unites States, and as chattel was "owned."* In the passage of time since this was a *reality* in America, the children of these African "slaves" (even the ones who are prisoners themselves) do not see the truth for what it really is. That *no* man, or *government of men*, can "own" another human being! So why did "slaves" believe this lie? And what happened in just one-hundred and twenty-nine years that obscures the lie of "ownership," from Black people's minds today?

Why does anyone think that the word "slave" is a *legitimate word*, describing Black people's imprisonment for over three-hundred years, when it is entwined with *"ownership" of that slave?* That was what I learned from my experience at Lorton, and by watching this large group of Black male prisoners. I realized that after so many years of imprisonment, a prisoner can become *"institutionalized"* into accepting the conditions of his incarceration. And, that the *real* world and its values, lose all meaning. It was all a lie, and brainwashing, to "institutionalize" the African prisoners!

Black "slaves" were *forced to believe* that another man could *own* them. *"Chattel" that was by American law, 'owned' by another human being.* I realized in Lorton that the word *'slave' was accepted as property* by Black people, but that a prisoner *was not.* A <u>prisoner</u> is "a man or woman, kept in custody, <u>captivity</u>, or a *<u>condition of forcible restraint</u>.*" None of them knew *or recognized* the differences between the *truth* and the *lie.* <u>That no man, can 'own' another man</u>! One can <u>only</u> hold the other as a <u>prisoner</u>. Finally, I had achieved a significant breakthrough. It had to do with the *mentality* of the whole group.

Prior to 1865, this mass of black-skinned prisoners, were *forced* to believe, that they were another man's *property. After* 1865 the *descendants* of these prisoner's, never having *been* 'slaves,' *continued* using a term they *cannot fathom* the significance of. All Black and White Americans today, *simply accept as <u>fact</u>, what they were 'taught.' The "fact"* that <u>dark-skinned human beings, **could be** and **were** *'property'*</u> *of white-skinned people'* I stated before, that Lorton prison was the largest predominately Black federal penitentiary in the United States, *and* it was almost *entirely self-sustaining.*

It operated its own dairy farm that produced wholesome milk and other dairy products. The convicts butchered their own meat, and farmed their own agricultural needs. And the industrial plants supplied everything from license plates for District of Columbia and Federal government automobiles, uniforms for the police and fire departments. Their industry constructed street signs, and did the major printing for all of the District governments' needs.

Uniforms for federal prisoners were fabricated there. Nine-thousand convicts operated a *massive* agricultural and industrial complex, almost without cost to the government.

Through Lorton, I began to understand how the South was able to amass such fortunes. But *at what cost* to the human beings that supplied the labor force? To lose one's perception of *human*-self is to become an *animal*. To Blacks and Whites in America today, the word "slavery" is an accepted reality of America's past "indiscretion." Both use the word as if it holds truth. Conclusion? One side is sick. The *other* side has *acquired* its sickness. White *and* Black folk think of *slavery* as a long period of the *forced ownership* of Black folk.

That *both* believe *ended* when Black people were *emancipated* by President Abraham Lincoln's order, and the Thirteenth Amendment. Something *happened* to *both* side's perception of the *truth,* concerning these *generations* of African people. Somehow, White Americans came to *believe* that *African prisoner's illegal captivity* had become *a just incarceration.* That there was a *legitimate* reason, for these Africans *and* their descendants, to be *held* by White-skinned Europeans and Americans. Incredibly, the *descendants of these prisoners themselves eventually acquired* the *same mentality!*

We began to describe *ourselves,* as *descendants of 'slaves!'* This is what is at the *root* of White America's *refusal* to *listen* to Black people's continued *requests* and *demands* for reparations. One side says "you were emancipated (*property-freed*), let it *go!*" The *other* side says "having been your former-*slaves (property-debt)*, you *owe* us *reparations!*" Neither side understands the truth. That Africans were *not* 'property.' They were *prisoners*, who had committed *no* crime. No one owes 'freed property,' an apology *or* reparations. Freedom is the 'reparation,' for a wild *animal*. Human beings unjustly imprisoned however, are *different*.

Prisoners held *unjustly* and against their will for over three-hundred years cannot be 'repaired,' with *just* their 'freedom.' Neither side *sees* the *truth*, because each 'side' has been *taught* to *believe* the lie. The word 'slave' has become an *integral* part of our shared 'culture,' and is the end-result of *hundreds* of years of programming. Try seeing things *my* way. I know that *African men and women were only prisoners*. They were prisoners *then, and their children are still prisoners now*. *"Institutionalized"* then *and their great-great grandchildren are "institutionalized" now!* My theory is that a "generational-institutionalization" is firmly in place.

WE HOLD THESE TRUTHS TO BE SELF EVIDENT...

Within the *sub*-culture created by prison life, there is *'institutionalization.'* It is a condition that affects *long-term* prisoners. They become so *used* to the conditions of their incarceration, that they cann*ot* easily function once they are released *back* into society. *Inside* of their prison, officers tell them *when* to do almost *everything*. They are told when to get up, when to eat, when they can have rec, when they can have visits, and when to go to bed. Imagine programming the *largest* group of prisoners *ever assembled*, to *accept* 'de-humanization' (slavery), *while incarcerated as prisoners*.

Now imagine <u>*generations*</u> *of this* <u>*same group of prisoners*</u>, *imprisoned* under these conditions for <u>*over three-hundred years*</u>! Then, these mentally broken *non-humans* are suddenly <u>*released*</u> from their imprisonment. Sent out into a 'civilized society,' without food, clothing, shelter, education, or protection. A *'society,'* that was *formed without them*. Only *they*, with *Black* skins, were *imprisoned* and *excluded* from this all-*White*-skinned society. After three-hundred years of captivity, *millions of Black-skinned de-humanized and mentally abused prisoners were being paroled within a larger group of White-skinned people*.

Into a *White* society which could *instantly recognize* the ex-'slaves' because of the *color* of *their* skins. These prisoners also had *two additional* and even *more serious handicaps* they were encumbered with. *The first was, that none of the Black-skinned prisoners released from this 'generational-captivity' were ever de-programmed from the lie that they were not human beings. The second was, that everyone in the White-skinned society into which they were now released, viewed them as all one united people!* Instead of as the large group of *different* people they were, *before* their imprisonment together *began!*

If conditions existing within prisons *create* 'institutionalized' behavior in *one* man's lifetime, what do you imagine would be the *end-result of generations of a prisoner group of this size?* Generations of *off-spring* of *the first 'group' of prisoners,* would be wretchedly broken and domesticated. Black people in America *today, are* the great-grandchildren of *generations* of these de-humanized Black-skinned people. A people who for over three-hundred years, suffered *unimaginable cruelty* at the hands of what had *become* "Americans."

The 'conditioning' that was required, to force Black people to accept their fate, reminded me of *other*

Americans who were subjected to a *similar* type of conditioning. Like many others I am an honorably-discharged Marine Corps veteran, of the Vietnam War. Do you remember that war? There were prisoners of that war, who suffered more than physical pain. There are stories of American P.O.W.'s, who had returned home in great mental anguish. The treatment that they had received while in the hands of their captors was tortuous.

Upon returning home, they had to undergo 'de-briefing,' and 'de-programming,' from this cruel 'conditioning' they had bravely survived. Through intense psychological therapy, many of them were able to rejoin their families and former lives. Many however, were *not* able to adjust to society. "Post Traumatic Stress Disorder,"(PTSD) is the term used to name the effects suffered by many of the survivors of that war. In another 'undeclared war,' *millions* of *different* Black-skinned people, were kidnaped and brought forcibly to the shores of America. They were tortured, broken in spirit, and used as *beasts of burden* by Europeans and Americans, for over three-hundred and sixty years. De-humanized, and devoid of any vestiges of a national identity, they were released into a hostile environment. They were mentally *incapable* of independent survival within a 'civilized-society' of Whites, who had for their entire captivity, ostracized their race. No people in recorded history, suffered as complete an erasure of their identity, as they. They were poor, illiterate as a whole, and had to quickly assimilate to survive in a hostile land. This was the sad history that marked my ancestor's 'freedom' in America.

That historical year, was for all intents and purposes, 1865. How much "psychological therapy" did this country give *them*, when *they* were finally released, from *their* captivity? As a prisoner-of-war must be 'de-programmed' from the conditions of his imprisonment, to live a normal life, so should *they* have been. Look at the amount of time given these broken people, to "straighten their backs." America *freed* them in 1865, and *then* made them *citizens*, in 1868. How could *anyone* in their right *minds*, expect this sick and separated group of *ex-property* to even *understand* the responsibilities of citizenship? "Post-Traumatic Stress Disorder?"

There *is* no term that can aptly describe *their* state of mind, after so *many* years of *this* brainwashing. Today, we are looking at each other, through a *mirage* of a 'slave.' We *both* see the same thing, through a *distorted* vision. When my ancestors were 'emancipated' from slavery, it only ended the unique conditions of their imprisonment. It did *nothing* to correct the *injustice of* that *act* of captivity. The government of the United States 'emancipated the slaves,' but no one *freed the prisoners*. Remember the experiment I conducted inside the prison and outside of it?

I asked Black people from each of the two different environments, to answer a question that each *should have known*. Yet, each group *did not realize that Black prisoners were "owned" by the government.* The words *slave* and *prisoner, held different meanings to them.* Do you remember the definition of *prisoner?* "A person kept in custody, **captivity**, ..or serving a prison sentence." *The word applies to both groups.* The government of this country *somehow* found a way to make an *injustice, justifiable. And found a way to make a lie, an accepted 'reason.'* Slave. It is the *mirage,* that today's Blacks *and* Whites actually *see.*

In reality, *millions* of these people were poorly-clad, hungry, abused, and mentally-challenged ex-prisoners. And *as any 'group' of prisoners, forced to live together and cooperate, were not one united people. Why,* hasn't America set the record straight, in all of these years? Quite simple. The government of the United States is the *will of the people of the United States.* If the *majority* of the people *wanted* change, it could have happened at *any* time. The United States Government could have been *ordered* to do this. They also should have been ordered to make a formal apology to the prisoners, for their *generations* of *unlawful captivity.*

Given them some offer of reparations *back then* in the form of land, money, and support from the government. America *could* have offered them free education, to bring the millions of illiterate people into civilization. America *could* have started a 're-education program' by law, to begin the massive healing process. One, reinforcing, that we are *all Americans.* We are one family with one destiny, with no color distinctions or prejudices. They *could* have *enforced* this law, with the full might of America's military, police, and courts. Finally, they *could* have created jobs for these excluded people, so they could be self-supporting. This was *not done*.

The government chose *instead*, to *ignore* them. *One-hundred and forty-eight years later*, the *majority* who *control* this government, *obviously still don't want these things to happen*. What will happen to us? As a separated group of 'institutionalized' prisoners, are we *regenerating* the conditions of our ancestor's captivity? Is this the *real* reason for our *fear*, and of our vicious *killing* of one another? Don't we realize that our 'group' *today* is comprised of the *children* of the *released dysfunctional prisoners of 1865? No, we don't*.

The *largest* group of *different* people *ever held together in North America as prisoners*, were *released* from a false imprisonment. The reason *for* their captivity was their Black skin. That was their 'crime.' But who really committed the crime of enslaving millions of people in this foreign land? The *colonists* committed a crime against people from the continent of Africa, and the *Americans* wiped it out of our combined memories. Gone. To be *replaced*, by a *non-crime*, America *named* "*Slavery.*"

ONE NATION, INDIVISIBLE, WITH LIBERTY AND JUSTICE, FOR ALL.

I am walking and thinking about all that I have uncovered. The ramifications of what America allowed to happen are enormous. 'Black' America today is *regenerating* the aberrations of *lifetimes* of mental and physical abuse through an untreated form of PTSD I call *"generational-institutionalization."* Without confronting the *truth* of this 'institutionalized' way of thinking and *correcting* it on *both* sides, Americans will *continue* to look at each other from *superior* and *inferior* viewpoints. Worse, we will continue to *subliminally* teach our *children*, to do the same thing.

An 'institutionalized' prisoner, that has been *conditioned to believe that he is property* that can be *owned* by another human being, is a spiritually and mentally *broken* human being. The idea that such *property* could be *'emancipated'* and *then* be given *citizenship, without being*

restored _to human status,_ is an idea only a madman could conjure. Since America abandoned us through segregation for almost one-hundred years, let's look at the _reality_ of _life,_ for these 'Negroes' _who have always been strangers to each other._ We _hate_ each other, because we _fear_ each other. Only White-skinned Americans, initially saw us as a _united_ group, by our skin-color.

Why did _this massive group of strangers,_ start referring to each other as '_us?_' It is an important part of the "institutionalization" process for prisoners. The 'group-mentality' of _prisoners_ is a natural by-product of forced "group-conditioning." Although _all_ of them are _different_ from one another, _because_ they _share_ the _same oppression and conditions,_ the 'group' refers to _itself_ as '_us._' Black-skinned people in America refer to _themselves_ as '_us,_' _simply because as America's prisoners of color,_ '_we_' _are still treated as 'one group.'_ Us against _them._

I have had my share of neglect and abuse reports. In the majority of cases, physical and mental abuse affects the victim for a _lifetime._ The _children_ of abused parents, witness _their_ abuse to each _other,_ and the _pattern_ of abuse becomes 'generational.' Through family, friends, a strong and loving community, and support from various medical professionals and programs, the abuse _can_ be stopped. However, _before_ the sickness can be _cured,_ it must _first be recognized._ Why, hasn't the Black community as a whole, recognized its own weaknesses? The _truth,_ as I realized inside Lorton prison, was _right in front of me._

The most _important_ reason why _Black_ people never

recognized our *own* sickness is because it had become an untreated part of our "institutionalized conditioning." It has been passed-down from "generation to generation," without abatement. Our sickness is evident. The *naming of us and our acceptance as "Black people," the fairy tale that we were "owned," as well as the belief that we are all <u>one people</u> because of our skin-color,* was part of the <u>*lie that was programmed* **into** *us as part of our 'slave' conditioning*</u>.

Africa is a *huge continent*, much the same as Europe. It contains different *nations, and* different *cultures* of people. Just because *two* people come from the same *continent,* does *not* mean that they are of the *same people.* The United States of America, in the beginning *and* now, was comprised of *many different nations of people.* The English, French, Spanish, Dutch, German, Irish, Scot, Portuguese, and Italian (to name a few), come from the *continent* of Europe. Africa *also* has Ghana, Nigeria, Ivory Coast, Liberia, Cameroon, Guinea, Sierra Leone, Senegal, and Benin (to name a few).

Each of these peoples, whether from the continent of Europe *or* the continent of Africa are a *sovereign people.* They come from nations, *different* from each other. The Europeans that established North America began populating this country from the early days of the first colonists until 1776 <u>*without*</u> laws <u>*uniting them.*</u> When the United States of America was created by the ratification of its Constitution, it did *more* than <u>unite the states.</u> It <u>*united*</u> the <u>*children*</u> of many *diverse* European <u>*nations*</u> into *one* <u>*new*</u> people. What was 'created,' was essentially a new and united *European people.*

These wise people *knew* that if left unchecked, the people *here* from *different* nations, would eventually *war* with each other. Like their *parent* nations had been doing in Europe for *thousands* of years. They *accepted as fact* what their black-skinned *prisoners* were *conditioned to forget. Nowhere* in the civilized world, do people care at *all* for their neighbors because their *skin-pigmentation is the same.* If *that* were the case, no European nations would *ever* have fought, because *they were all White-skinned.* Neither would the Native Americans have fought, tribal nation against tribal nation.

Everyone would simply have said, *"we are the same skin-color, why are we fighting?"* The United States became the *only* nation in the world, to bring together under *one* flag, *all of the children of 'White-skinned' European nations.* A truce was formed *here*, between the children of these many diverse European nations. The dark-skinned people from the African continent (who built this nation) *were excluded*, the people from the continent of China (who later built the railroads) *were excluded*, Native-Americans (whose land was taken from them) *were excluded*, and the Central American people from Mexico (whose land was also taken) *were excluded.*

Americans *love* "colors" of skin. Well, if you *exclude Black, Yellow, Brown and Red from your world, what color do you have left?* So, the United States of America in 1789 was a *melting-pot* of diverse European nations, and all of them *learned to live together as one* through a *constitutional agreement*. So began an experiment where *White*-skinned people from many different *European* nations, *voluntarily* co-existed by a written agreement. This majority wrapped around a massive group of *Black*-skinned people from different *African* nations, *forced to co-exist, without any written agreement whatsoever*.

Once you free the 'slaves,' *what keeps them* 'together' and controlled? Only a *continuation* of their *shared oppression could* continue to bind and control them. The *White* citizens of the United States of America knew *even in* 1789 that the *mutual* coloring of their *skins* was *not enough* to *prevent* them from one day *killing* each other. *Why* didn't America allow it's *freed 'slaves'* of the *same skin color*, the opportunity to become *a sovereign people themselves, before* enclosing *all* of them *under their constitution?* Fear that *united,* we might wage *war* against them? That is quite possible, but I believe there is a simpler answer.

America *arrogantly* never *considered* the *possibility* that these *'falsely united Black people' they had created through 'slavery,'* would *need* a reason to *legally bind* one to the other, once 'slavery' ended. Just as *they had done,* not quite one-hundred years earlier. From a massive group of diverse Europeans, *they created* "E Pluribus Unum," or *"out of many, one."* Put another way, what if the "U.S. Constitution" was torn in two by the people of the United States. What do you think all *White-skinned* people, would eventually *do to each other, here?*

Remember, once you destroy what keeps them

united, you *also* disband *all of the police and military that keep that unity protected. There would be anarchy. Without a constitution* to formally bind *ourselves,* can you understand *now,* why 'Black *people'* are *killing themselves? Who among* us, was given the *authority* **by** us, to stop this? We have no *enforcement for our combined will.* Without our *own law, there is no way to stop ourselves from self-destruction. Exactly* like prisoners within a prison.

As an officer, I am *sworn* to uphold and defend, the *Constitution of the United States.* In other words, I am *empowered by Whites* to uphold the Constitution which binds *them* together in America, while *ignoring* the fact that **my** people **have** *no such 'constitutional binding' for themselves. No sovereign people in the free world* are *one* because *someone else* said that they were. And, *none* of these people have named *themselves* or *been named,* a *color.* It is a dangerous reality that is not recognized, nor rationally dealt with. We are a 'prisoner-group,' who *should be united, but legally are not.*

White people and *Black* people. Are we all *forever ingrained, as color-activated racists!* One side, *created* this sickness. The other side *is infected* with it. Is this a *permanent* part of us? Can we heal ourselves, and our children of this?

A DREAM FROM THE PAST

The body of students, faculty, and reporters settled into their seats as the speaker took his place at the podium. He had been invited to this prestigious university, to speak to the young leaders of America about racism in the United States. His eyes slowly swept the assemblage, and he gestured to a young collegiate in the front row. "I would like to conduct an experiment, would you be so kind as to assist me?" he asked the bright-eyed youth. "Yes, sir," came the immediate reply. "I will name the country, and I would like you, to name the *color* of the people living there. Do you think that you can do this" he asked? The student answered again, "Yes, sir." He wasted no time, but proceeded very quickly.

"Nigeria" (speaker)
"Black" (student)

"Russia" (speaker)
"White" (student)
"Mexico" (speaker)
"Brown" (student)
"China" (speaker)
"Yellow" (student)

He thanked the student for his cooperation, and then asked him to reverse roles and offer the same questions to him. The student agreed. Unconsciously, the body leaned forward to hear.

"Nigeria" (student)
"Any color" (speaker)
"Russia" (student)

"Any color," the speaker said again, staring intently at the white student, as if hoping.

"Mexico" (student)

"Any color. Brown, Black, Red, White, and Yellow-skinned people, live in Mexico" he said.

"The color of one's skin *cannot be used* to *visually* predict or dictate one's *nationality*. Only Americans believe it to be so." Then, he looked directly into the student's eyes and said, "What if I had asked, 'the <u>United States of America?</u>' Would you have responded, *White*?" the speaker asked the student. With that, the red-faced student said very softly, "I understand, sir."

Malcolm X smiled warmly, and shook his hand.

...IN ORDER TO FORM A MORE PERFECT UNION...

Black, White, Negro, Colored. Terms established as *identifiers* of each group *generations* before I was born. Descriptions of human-beings, intended to *visually* identify, two *groups* of *different* people. We use these descriptions, automatically and unconsciously, as we have *all* been *trained* to do. Eye contact, and 'click,' *he's* 'White' and *she's* 'Black.' Is this '*color-racism*' that was created and perpetuated by long-dead Europeans and Americans, which *still infects <u>this</u> generation of Americans today, too deep in our souls* to be cured?

Whether intentional or not, in 1789, America created a united European union called "the United States of America." Its *purpose,* as <u>stated</u> in the Constitution, says:

"We the People of the United States, in Order

to form a more perfect Union, establish Justice, insure domestic Tranquility, provide for the common defence, promote the general Welfare, and secure the Blessings of Liberty to ourselves and our Posterity, do ordain and establish the Constitution for the United States of America."

This document is one of the most brilliant legal documents ever written. It created a *sovereign* people. It has been copied by many countries in the world since it was written. People used its wisdom to unite *themselves* under their *own* constitutions. *"One nation, Indivisible,..."* Yet, for all of its wisdom, it is obvious that its *intent* was *selective*. The people who *created this document* in 1776, did *not* extend its coverage to *Black-skinned people, until 1868*. Many of them that signed this document, *owned 'slaves' themselves.*

We became the *only* people in the history of Mankind, to be *excluded* from a nation's founding laws, simply because of the *color of our skins. This* is the reason I say the Thirteenth, Fourteenth, and Fifteenth Amendments are hollow. The three descriptions covered by these Amendments, are named 'party,' 'persons,' and 'citizens.' *Chattel*, cannot in a *human* sense, *ever* be 'party,' 'persons,' or 'citizens.' To go from human being, to prisoner, then to 'slave,' was an established *norm* in America.

To *emancipate* the *slave,* instead of *freeing* the *prisoner,* turns a *crime,* into a *benevolent action.* I view this as an unsatisfactory and mean-spirited *dismissal.* There was no *closure*, for those Black-skinned 'slaves,' *or their generations.* And for those *'slaves'* and *their* generations to have *accepted* this condition of 'freedom,' *proves* that the sickness *is ingrained forever into our mentality.* Both groups have found a way, to *legitimize* a crime. As if there were *grounds* for the incarceration. It was an illegal act that America legitimized forever, by granting 'emancipation' status to.

The President of the United States *may* grant emancipation, or manumit *convicted criminals* who are being *pardoned* of a crime. This is a power given him by Article Two, section two, of the Constitution. What *crime* did *we* commit, as a Black-skinned group, that *required* Presidential reprieve or pardon? And once 'freed,' did *anyone* give thought to the fact, that these Black-skinned *prisoners* were *not one people?* You see, all of these White-skinned colonists in 1776, came together to create a *whole* people out of what *had been separate.*

The *millions* of Black people that were now *'free'* from *'slavery,'* had *also* been *separated* from *their different* homelands *and* from each *other,* by the conditions of their *captivity.* In addition, they had been *in-bred against their will,* over a period of *three-hundred years.* The result of which, created a *new* race of African people. A new race in *fact,* but not legitimized by *themselves,* in *deed.* "Out of many, one." Who asked *our* permission, before *enclosing* us *forever* as a *separated* group, under *this* Constitution? *"..In order to form a more perfect Union."* There *are* no such people, as BLACK people. This is *only* a description.

We never had the *chance* to make of *ourselves,* one new people. This racist colonial mentality of one *united* 'Negro' *without law* has *got* to stop. *We* need *also,* to insure 'domestic tranquility' among *ourselves.* We need *also,* to establish 'Justice' among *ourselves.* We, need *also,* to provide for *our* 'common defense and to promote our general Welfare.' These *most* important rights, privileges, and liberties, have been *denied* an entirely *new* race of people, who *need* them to survive. Ironically, they have been denied *by* the race of people who *used* these *same powers* to unite *themselves.*

After unification by your *own* laws, *you* covered *our* confused and separated new race with *your* constitution. *You* may enforce *your* law upon *us,* but *we* cannot make or enforce laws upon *ourselves.* This is the greatest *in-*justice *done* to this color-caste and de-humanized group of Black people. To have *accepted* this 'adoption,' leading to a future of self-immolation, is *proof enough* that my ancestors were suffering from their *abuse.* Today, my new race is the *only* one in the world, which *has* no *constitutional binding* for *all* of its parts. *Think about this.* Everyone *else* here, became Americans from some *place,* while *we* became Americans from some-*thing.*

"Master' *gave* us some of *his* 'constitution,' so *we* don't *need* any for *ourselves."* This was the subtlety of the Fourteenth Amendment. The White majority do as they please with us. Without our *own constitution, or help from those that control the one we owe allegiance to,* we are *destroying* each other. We, as a *people* and *not* ex-

property, must make up our minds to _what_ shall we remain true? Remain true to an _adopted_ citizenship that _denies_ us _true_ self-control? Or do we _acknowledge_ what has _happened_ to us to _keep_ us separated, and _correct_ that action to _become_ whole? _Will_ White Americans, _help_ correct the sins of their fore-fathers?

This is the burning question that I am asking America. _Who_ will take responsibility for the crimes committed against my people? No White man answers. Each of them washes their hands of the responsibility. Records are lost, and memories have dimmed. They say that there are very _few_ amongst them today that will admit to being _directly descended_ from the _slave owners_ of yesteryear. They are _adamant_ that as a country, _they_ owe _this Black group nothing_ more than any other citizens. I would have to agree, if I were viewed simply as _an American,_ by them.

There is only _one_ small problem with that. I am _not_ viewed "simply" as an "American" by them! Every White person I interviewed for my research, I asked, _"what do you think is my nationality?"_ Each and _every_ response was "**Black**-American." Or they would answer "**African**-American." Not _one White person,_ answered simply _"an American."_ I did not become angry, because I understood. I simply pointed out to them that as _they_ see all Black people in America as "one _Black people,_" _we_ see _them_ as "one _White people,_" who _by law are all responsible for each other_.

The instant all of you became "one people" by law you _assumed_ the criminal actions of those _who had once been_ *singularly responsible* for their abominable behaviors. When *all of you* voluntarily agreed to a constitutional binding, and *intentionally excluded the Black man and woman*, *you all became responsible* for the actions of the few. Or *someone* is *lying*. So, how shall we continue our 'relationship,' America? It does not do any good to shrug off responsibility for the actions of *other* White-skinned people taken in the past. Those actions were taken by *the 'colonists' who later became Americans*.

This is your initial constitutionally-*united* group of "Forefathers." Do not try *now*, to *absolve* yourselves, of the *responsibilities* of your *citizenship*. You must *all* correct the *mistakes* of this nation's past. Do not obfuscate *further*. *You*, the *silent majority*, can start to *heal* our *combined* sickness. To *prove* to your *'pardoned-prisoners,'* that our future *together* has hope. What, are *you* going to do? If your ever silent *response* is your steadfast *refusal* to direct this great republican machine *you* control in the right direction, then you will *all cement* the past 'American' injustice.

You, the majority, will *continue to prove by your apathy* that there are *two* kinds of American. Black and White. Instead of being *a part* of America, you will force us from sheer *neglect*, to *remain* a shunned 'Black' group. And *to these people*, these *separated* 'Black' people, *your* 'constitution' becomes *a lie*. Black and White. Together *finally*, or continued *separation*, forever? 'Black' America *desperately* needs help. We are *killing* each other. We *fight* amongst each other. We have adopted *'classes,'* amongst each other. We are *trampling* each other, as *prisoners do* inside of their prison.

Our poor *have* no recourse, but to commit crime to survive in the ghettoes. The illusion of freedom since 'integration,' has allowed those among us who possess exceptional *assimilation* skills, to try to *escape* their 'Black' prison. We run from each other to the suburbs. Did we successfully 'escape?' No. Too late, we all discover, that *there is no escape from being 'Black.'* The aberrations of our conditions of captivity continue *unabated* in <u>all</u> of 'our' communities. Who will stop it? *Are we truly 'one nation indivisible,'* or are we *two* nations? *One 'indivisible,' and the other, <u>invisible?</u>*

Must we continue to be a 'separate but *un*-equal' people, who *must* find a way, to prevent our own genocide?

THE MILLION-MAN MARCH

It's like pulling an errant string, on the sleeve of your sweater. It gets longer, and longer, and before you know it, you are unintentionally *unraveling* your sweater. The more I examined my ancestor's past, and its *effects* upon them, the more questions arose. The more answers I found, the more questions came to mind. What if "America" isn't *listening* to what I have written? What if, Black and White Americans *don't* find a way to stop the lies, and *truly* become <u>one</u> *people under a <u>united</u> constitution?* What will happen to all of us?

Let's take a look at an anomaly that was the precursor for what America *will see again*. Our false 'unity,' is starting to dissolve. What *really* was behind, the *"Million Man March?"* I believe that the 'march' consisted of separated groups of *'nationally-cleansed'* Africans, *subliminally* looking *desperately* for *some* way to *unite*. As did the diverse children of different

European nations, who found themselves suddenly free from the yoke of England, but *recognized* their instant vulnerability.

They came from nations on a *continent* that *had been warring with each other for centuries.* If some sort of legal *unification* was not forthcoming, their futures together would be in jeopardy. Whether the idea came from Washington, Jefferson, Madison, Adams, Hamilton, Jay, or Ben Franklin, it does not make any difference. *Some* genius *among* them saw a glimpse of the future. "We *must* find a way, to *unite* ourselves, or *anarchy* will *eventually* be our children's future." A *'United States of America,'* was proposed in 1776 by the original Articles of Confederation, and eventually the constitution was made into law in 1789.

Instead of being *a separated group* of diverse national origins, with different cultures and backgrounds, they melded themselves into *a sovereign people.* As the "Euro-dollar" combined the currencies of most of Europe into one interchangeable standard, so *these* children of diverse European nationalities merged *themselves* into *one new "American" standard.* Since the White *woman was denied* a vote, the concerned White *men* met in the 'Capitol' of those times. Would you imagine *maybe one-million of them gathered together to discuss such an important event?* Were these White men, of *different* religions, politics, and cultures?

Did this 'gathering,' produce the impetus, for their *legal unification* as a *sovereign* 'nation' of people? Now, let's take a *good* look at what happened at the 'Million-

Man March,' in 1995. Did the largest number of Black-skinned men *ever* assembled in *one* place at *one* time, since we were brought to this land, occur in *this* nation's 'Capitol?' Were you there? It was *magnificent!* Every shade and complexion of our 'Black' world was represented that day. But, after a very long day of speeches and sharing, what did 'we' accomplish? Did we present the idea of a constitutional unification and sovereignty, for *'ourselves and our posterity?'*

Did we talk about creating *laws* that would *punish* those of our 'new' united people, who *hurt* us? No. We did not. Instead, we made 'promises.' Which of course having no *legal enforcement, we could not keep.* Yet, I wonder? Didn't <u>*some*</u> White Americans *instinctively* <u>*know*</u>, what *could* have happened to 'Black America' on that day? Didn't *they* commit to the *identical* action, two-hundred and nineteen years *earlier? Of course, they did!* So, why didn't the *natural course of our legal unification* become a reality that day?

Even though the *actions* of the 'group' <u>*simulated*</u> an aggressive unification and possible *secession* from the United States, *the members of that group were <u>never informed</u> <u>of the true spirit of their gathering</u>.* That was kept from them, I believe, intentionally. Instead, the *picture* of these million 'Black' men was broadcast world-wide, as a *warning to White America of what <u>could</u> be done.* I believe this whole concerted action was to *threaten* White America, for some hidden agenda, oblivious to the crowd. Total euphoria blinded the participants that day.

The joy of seeing that many of each other in the same place for the first time, made even the most *educated and assimilated* among them, temporarily *forget* how this gathering would be viewed. Viewed by their 'masters,' who had done the *same* thing, to become a sovereign people. Let me break this down further. I have explained the truth about the word "slave." It is a fictional character made *real*, by the cold-blooded cruelty of White-skinned Europeans and Americans. So *too*, is the fiction that *all Black-skinned 'savages,'* come from some indistinguishable *'Black nation'* called *"Africa."*

This racist and colonial mentality, has survived amongst White-skinned Americans for centuries. In truth, what 'came out' of slavery in 1865, *was not what went into* this insane period of our captivity. Through the forced mixing of our *once*-sovereign nationalities and tribes, a *thoroughly 'mixed' new African emerged*. A people who were *the same skin color*, but *through 'domestication' had forgotten that they were no longer of one tribe or nation*. Sovereignty *unites a people*. It makes that people *independent*. The action of becoming sovereign *makes the world acknowledge you as a nation of people*.

We have no respect. Not amongst ourselves as a whole, _or_ from the rest of the nations of people of the world. When Europeans visit 'White America,' they subliminally *acknowledge* the miracle of a *European cooperative in effect*, here. No *matter* their differences in Europe, when they step off of the plane or ship *here*, there is a *'truce' in effect! They are safe here, even* if two

European countries are <u>at war with each other</u>. When 'Black-skinned' sovereign people visit 'Black America,' they land in *the 'Twilight Zone.'* Many of them, *don't* understand what is *wrong* with us?

It is because they *assume* that *we Black Americans are a <u>sovereign people</u>.* And *like* the White Europeans that visit White America, *think* that they are *safe* here, *amongst a 'united' Black-skinned people. <u>They are so wrong</u>.* We rob them, and murder them. We are mean to them, and ostracize them. Instead of *welcoming* them, we slander them. *They ask the same question, "why?" It is because 'we' are only a separated prisoner 'group.'* We have our prison 'cliques.' We don't *have* a legal unity. We *only* have the color of our skins. After a while, these Black-skinned visitors are *ashamed* to be with us here.

In a short while, *they <u>see</u> the insincerity of our words.* *They* do not label each other 'Black,' where they come from. Nor do they call themselves "nigger." They respond with anger towards those of us who *do* these things to them. Why? *This is the reason.* America is the richest and most powerful nation in the world. Everyone who visits sees *only* what our propaganda has *taught* them. They are not aware, of the reality of life in America for Black-skinned people. They are blinded by America's potential. They take their *own* sovereignty *<u>for granted</u>.*

<u>Having</u> a legal unification with others of their nation, they <u>cannot see</u> what <u>we</u> are <u>missing</u> here. These visitors have been 'caught-up,' in the lie *that Americans* have legitimized, that all 'Black' people are 'brothers'

and 'sisters.' First and foremost, you must have *constitutional* unity. *Then,* you can invite all *other* Black-skinned people to your unified table, to equally share your bread. Our unification, simply *because* of our Blackness, is wrong. The 'founding Fathers' of America, knew this. The *false* reason for *our* unification, is crumbling. Why?

The 'color' of a man's skin, does *not* automatically guarantee his safety, with a like-hued man. What is his nationality? I *don't* think the majority of the 'Black' men present at the 'March,' *really knew what* the need was, that called them to come together. I do. It was the irrepressible *need* to *form* themselves into *one sovereign people* that called *out* to them. 'We' are *killing* each other. 'Black' men are abandoning their children, and leaving the 'Black' woman, to shoulder the weight of both parents. 'We' are not respectful of one another, or our women. 'We' have acquired low morals, and 'we' advertise this ignorance, to the world.

'We' substitute our *religions* as the *focal* point of our lives, *instead* of respecting *one another's religious preferences,* and *still* loving ourselves as *one united people.* America, *can* 'Black' people *ever be able peacefully, to consolidate their different parts into one?* Does the 'constitution' that binds us together forever, *forbid our* 'group' *covered by it* from forming our *own 'constitutional' agreement while under it? If so, then eventually our two groups will one day, face each other.* The 'Million-Man *and* Woman' march, is destined to come to you *again.*

Your refusal to fully integrate your society with us, as well as your blatant and hidden racism, will eventually cause us to look amongst ourselves for our own solutions. After exhausting all other avenues, and failing, we will seek the only possible solution. Black people, *must* do something *ourselves,* for our *own* self-preservation.   Remember again, and again, your ancestor's words.   "In order to form a more perfect Union....?" History always repeats itself, and the hour of our unification is fast approaching.

"Negro," is the name of a race, as is "Caucasian." It *does not* specify one's nationality. This is the 'fork in the road,' for *all* of us. Do we become one *united* people, or must Black people accidentally or intentionally, come together under *our* *own* constitution? Must we one day, shake-off that which *binds us,* as *your* ancestors once did with England? Once we awaken to the truth of our combined sickness, we may *then* start to heal ourselves. As long as we all stay focused on the absurd, the *real issues*, are *never* going to be resolved. The issues of violence, poverty, homelessness, hunger, joblessness, and *racism, affect us all.*

Racism is *not* dead. It is alive and well, and surrounds us all. Just because *you* don't practice it, or even *see* it, doesn't mean that it's gone. The dangers of our past are still real. We are a *very* sick people. We *can cure ourselves, if we want.*   We can only do it, one problem at a time. First, and foremost, is to recognize what happened to us as a people. Black-skinned and

White-skinned. This is not about 'who is right,' and 'who is wrong.' It is about understanding what happened in our past, to correct what we feel now, in the present. Otherwise, a 'Million-Man' march is going to be the *least* of your worries.

I needed to walk again. I have been un-raveling this 'sweater,' for a long time. Question. Answer. More questions. More answers. Walking sometimes helps me clear my mind. With all of this thinking, I was walking a lot, lately.

BLACK FOLK'S PLIGHT IN D.C.

Lorton Reformatory is now closed forever. The District of Columbia and the Federal Government have decided its fate. After ninety-one years, it finally ceased operations in December of 2001. I am now working in the Receiving and Discharge (R&D) area of the District's only jail. It is named the "Central Detention Facility." Recently, court orders restricting the number of men and women to be held here were lifted. Our District government-run jail is connected by an over-head walkway, to another building named the "Central Treatment Facility."

This edifice used to belong wholly to the District government, to treat the many drug-addicts incarcerated at the jail. It also held our female inmates, prisoners going through classification. The District found operating such a massive jail system, too fiscally demanding. There was a growing push on, to allow the privatization of our jail system, to help alleviate the financial burden. A private correctional service out of Memphis, Tennessee, came to the rescue. The "Corrections Corporation of America," was given a "sale-lease back" agreement, to take-over our Central Treatment Facility.

It operates side-by-side, with the District of Columbia Department of Corrections. A private prison and government jail that shuttles prisoners back and forth on a daily basis. The 'D.C. Jail,' as the Central Detention Facility is still known to all, holds a daily population of approximately two-thousand, three-hundred men and women. The Central Treatment Facility, or "C.T.F.," holds approximately nine-hundred men and women. Every male incarcerated in the District of Columbia, whether they go to the C.T.F., or stay at the jail, eventually comes by *me* in Male Receiving and Departure. We like to call it "Male R&D."

Over a period of years, I have noticed certain *patterns* in the population of pre-trial detainees that warranted closer examination. I will give you an example. Of the roughly three-thousand, two-hundred men and women incarcerated today at the Jail and C.T.F., there are *only* approximately *one-hundred White* people in *both* buildings. Further, *of* these thirty-two hundred men and women, there are only approximately two-hundred *new numbers*. Let me explain what I mean, when I say "new-numbers." The District of Columbia Department of Corrections, issues *each* person that comes into the jail, an armband.

On this arm-band, is printed a six-digit identification number. That number *stays with you for the rest of your life.* If you are *ever* locked-up by the police, and ordered to the jail by the courts, *that same number* will be *re-issued* to you. Time, and time, again. So when I say that there are only approximately two-hundred *new* numbers in the jail, what I am *really* saying, is *over three thousand people under my custody have been here before.* The number currently, is almost three-hundred and five *thousand* series. That's correct.

In a city whose population is almost fifty-percent Black, or roughly two-hundred and fifty-thousand Black people, the *'one-time only' arm-band number is over 305,000 issued.* And considering the *enormous* disparity between the numbers of Blacks and Whites incarcerated, *that number exceeds* the *total* number of Black people that *live* in the District of Columbia. *That includes all men, women, and children.* The numbers represent every person ever incarcerated in the system since they began issuing criminal record numbers back in the 1940's.

Drug abuse, violent crimes of passion, drug-selling and possession, gun possession or crimes committed with a hand-gun, are among the *top* reasons our felons are incarcerated. They are the "cream" of our jail population. The *majority* of our prisoners are incarcerated for general societal infractions. Drunk driving, no permit, drinking in public, parole violators, panhandling, simple assault, disorderly conduct, contempt of court, failure to pay child-support, etc. They run the gambit of society's ills. However, based on the number of cases that are constant *recidivists,* I faced a startling fact. My *pay*check was *dependent* upon these constant recidivists.

Indeed, without *them,* nearly everyone in the entire criminal justice system in the District of Columbia would be *literally* out of a job! Remember that I told you earlier, that I have the honor of being the *only* officer to have worked *all* of the areas of law enforcement in the District? I have served as a police officer, a federal marshal in the courts, and now as a corrections officer. My unique perspective *allowed me to see a complete picture that no other officer could see, of the effects of the criminal justice system on Black people here.* Look at the numbers of people that are involved in "herding" Black people on the 'plantation' of D.C.

There are approximately six-thousand police officers in the District (all branches). There are almost one-hundred and fifty judges and magistrates between the D.C. Superior Court and the U.S. District Court (with judges serving on *both* Courts of Appeal). There are approximately one-hundred Deputy United States Marshals, for all of the courts. There are approximately one-thousand Department of Corrections' and CTF officers, and two-hundred juvenile officers. That means to complete the 'circle' of the criminal justice system in the District it takes a *minimum* of **seven-thousand four-hundred** *uniformed* *officers of the people, to* **control** *this system.*

That number does *not include* the over four-thousand *civilians* that *support us* in our daily tasks. Combined, over *eleven-thousand people* <u>depend upon the</u> <u>three-thousand two-hundred people locked-up in the system</u>, *for their survival.* The District government's heartfelt entreaties to end the violence in the face of these statistics cannot be sincere. In reality, it *needs* these lock-ups. It *wants* these lock-ups. It subliminally *encourages,* these lock-ups. Otherwise, almost *everyone* would *lose* his or her *job* that keeps this criminal justice system humming.

Police, the overwhelming majority of whom patrol the *Black* side of Washington, would be unemployed. The District of Columbia is rather unique. As the Nation's Capitol, we are *subordinate* to Congress, and therefore remain under Congressional oversight. As a federal enclave, we *have* no 'Sheriff's Department.' Our local court system is protected by Deputy U.S. Marshals, who would lose many of *their* jobs without the District's Black criminals. How many *judges* would you need, if 'Black' people were not being incarcerated? To judge only 100 *White* criminal cases, in a one-month period?

How many Correctional Officers would you need in the *jail,* for only 100 *White* prisoners in a month's period of time? The point I am making is that without the *active cooperation* of *'Black'* people here in the District continuing their *pattern* of criminal behavior, a major portion of the criminal justice system would *simply shut-down.* How in the world, did this system, *get* this way you might ask? I believe the District government both *allowed* and *encouraged it* to grow to this magnitude for an obvious reason. Here is how it all began.

During the period of segregation in the District, Whites and Blacks were *legally separated.* For one-hundred years since 1865, Black people were *forced* to live amongst ourselves and survive, interdependently. We perpetuated the illusion of being one people, because the greater majority who controlled us all, *viewed us as one.* In our forced living together, we *had to* "police" ourselves. This was the District that my grandfather, my father and I, grew up in. From the 1920's through the 1960's, the *accepted* way of life for the *majority* of 'Black' people, was segregation. Each "side" made sure that things stayed quiet and orderly.

From the late sixties, to the mid-seventies, *real* integration came into 'Black' people's lives and everything changed. A sub-cultural phenomenon occurred almost overnight in 'Black' America, and had a profound effect on crime. As I mentioned earlier, the Blacks with money and education moved to the suburbs. The poor and un-educated, with few exceptions, remained. Poverty and ignorance *breed* social disorder. *This* is what our neighborhoods became nationwide. Places where violence and chaos slowly escalated. In the District, that meant an escalation of personnel for the police, courts, and jail/prison. Money was to be made, and a lot of it.

Then, President Nixon declared a "war on drugs." Between the drug dealers and the police, we are surrounded. A 'siege-mentality' has now *replaced* our feelings of *safety* within our own 'communities.' No day passes, that some violent act does not play itself out in once-quiet neighborhoods. What is the government's reaction? More *law enforcement,* of course. 'Business,' remember? The 'first responders' to escalating violence, are the police. Do you think that they are all out there, to *protect* you? Let me give you a view from *my* perspective.

Washington, D.C., was almost exclusively 'Black' on one side, and 'White' on the other. This is changing, as 'Whites' scramble to re-take their Nation's Capitol. Despite the apparent changes, for most 'Black' people the lines of demarcation *still* remain. On the 'White' side of the District, there is only <u>one</u> *police District,* to enforce the law for 'Whites.' On the *'Black'* side of the District, there are <u>six</u> *police Districts, patrolling 'our' neighborhoods.* Of the over three-thousand, five-hundred police officers of the Metropolitan Police Department, over *two-thousand five-hundred officers* patrol on the *Black* side of the District.

One would think that with *that many* sworn police officers in little more than *half of the populated city,* that the crime-rate would eventually be zero. Not so. There is very little police/community interaction, where the rewards of working together, result in less crime. Where the knowledge of the people you protect, and who are your neighbors, pays dividends in *how* you patrol. That's not going to happen until the demographics change. That is because *very few of these officers, live in the areas they patrol.* This is only a good paying *job* to them, not a place they want to live. The city once tried to make them live here for the job. I said "tried."

The police department always maintained a strong union. They were able to convince the Congressmen and Senators from the surrounding jurisdictions in which *they* live, to *stop* the District government from keeping this proposed regulation. The District government, being an obedient servant to the Congress, quietly rescinded this proposal. So, a loosely enforced "twenty-five mile rule," is the order of the day. That meant, that officers were allowed to live up to twenty-five miles, away from the Capitol building.

I personally knew of only *twenty* White police officers that I served with, who obeyed this "rule." Earlier, I told you that for *some* White officers, the District is a *very* good paying job. Here, is what I meant. Though a large percentage of police officers on the D.C. Police Department are *White*, they are *not* rushing, to all work on the *White* side of town. This is the side of town that has only *one* police station. The Second District is located on Idaho Avenue. No. The majority of these *White* officers, work on the *Black* side of town.

And *many* of them work between six p.m., and six

a.m. Hmmm...*why* would a *White* man from Des Moines, Iowa, even *want* to be a police officer, working on the *Black* side of the District of Columbia in the evening and at night? Here is the reason. The District of Columbia is one of the *few* Metropolitan cities with a population of this size, to have *no night court*. Our court system pretty much closes down, *at sundown*. So, if you happen to be a police officer with an arrest *after 5 p.m.* when the *court is closed*, you will have to 'paper' that arrest during normal *daytime* court hours.

Since your *normal* hours of duty are *after the court closes for the day*, your appearance in court to *start* the long road for your prisoner to walk is *overtime*. And, so is your appearance for each and every ordered 'come-up,' of your prisoner's walk through the court system during the day. Where *you* as the arresting officer *may be needed to testify*, about little things the court may have questions about concerning 'your arrest.' If you are a *very* busy police officer, with quite a few felony arrests, it is *quite* possible for you to earn in excess of <u>*one-hundred thousand dollars per year*</u> in salary <u>*and*</u> overtime. *Does this sound like a "bounty" system for catching Blacks?*

As the 'Receiving and Discharge' officer at the jail, I eventually see *all* of the prisoners the police lock-up, and that the courts send to jail. *The entire jail and CTF holds less than 100 White men, out of three-thousand and two-hundred people?* Ask yourself as I have, are *all* of the *White* people in the District of Columbia obeying *all* of the laws, *all of the time?* Or more realistically, are *most of the police only looking on the Black side of town for perpetrators?* How can they help *not* arresting so many Black people, when <u>six</u> of the <u>seven</u> police Districts are <u>all</u> <u>located</u> on the <u>Black</u> *side of the city?*

The government of the District of Columbia *knows* this. With a Black Mayor, Black City Council-members in half of these predominately Black wards, one-hundred Black top-ranked police officials in these areas, *and* Black Neighborhood Advisory Commissioners, there is no excuse for the continuation of this plantation mentality. With nothing legally to bind us together, Black folk *contribute* to our own oppression. Let's look at another way *we* hurt <u>ourselves</u>. Foremost is the breakdown of the Black family in the District of Columbia.

A great *majority* of single-families are being run absent the father. The proliferation of drugs and guns in the Black community, keeps the numbers of deaths steady. There also is an increasing trend of hiring 'out-of-towners,' for the most lucrative city jobs. *They* in turn, seek only the Black 'elite,' for *their* staff. Employment figures *are* good, but the positions filled are *increasingly* by people who live *outside of the District.* Also, the *reluctance* of these 'elite,' to hire ex-cons, *insures* a *steady* number of parole violators, and criminal recidivists.

Much of the young Black population fails to understand that their criminal conviction (slavery) follows them for the rest of their adult life. The high unemployment rate among young Black men and women, who are making more and more babies, *keeps* them living on or below the levels of poverty. All of these factors, and many more, *contribute* to the pain felt in our communities. It is my belief that this bureaucracy, looks upon this misery as an <u>*excuse*</u>. Only as an excuse for this bloated government, to keep operating at full capacity.

The *reason* that the Black community is under siege, is that *there is no 'we,' and the government of the United States <u>does not care</u>.* Since 1865, with the enactment of the Thirteenth Amendment, it *has never <u>really</u> cared about Black people's concerns, because it <u>still views us as</u>* **a '*Black*'** *group of people. Why not 'control' us, and keep American industry working at the same time?* Go to the Spring Valley section of D.C., at night, and just listen. It used to be like this in *every* neighborhood in the District, *before* integration. Remember?

Now, everyone I meet says they *used* to live in the neighborhood. They have moved *out* of D.C. but they still *work* in the District. Thousands of them and *still*, the problems worsen. The needs of our communities are met with apathy in almost every department. To these "drive-in" workers, this is *also*, only a job. We need people who <u>*live*</u> *here* to come <u>*forward*</u> and help the <u>*citizens*</u> living *here*. Ex-cons *need* jobs, housing, and money to *survive*. They have families, too. Teachers, in D.C. Public Schools, need *support*. They are being *forced* to be fathers, mothers, police officers, counselors, and suppliers of their *own* work materials.

In a city of over 600,000 people, that has a $9.5

billion budget, there _is_ no excuse. District government agencies need _real_ managers and Directors, who _know_ and _care_ about their workers, as _well_ as _the public that they serve._ Not 'drive-by' Directors, who stay _just_ long enough to _enhance their resume's and pocket ridiculously high salaries._ The separation of Whites and Blacks, from 1865 to 1965, _solidified_ 'Black' America. The _additional_ separation of 'Blacks' who _have_ from 'Blacks' who _have not since_ 1965, is exposing _a hierarchy within_ a _sub-_culture.

It is the one that I am most familiar with. The third 'circle' of convicts. It is _this_ hierarchy of long-term prisoners that I witnessed _inside of the Lorton Prison._ This predatory world of self-hatred and violence is growing. There are more _poor_ 'Black' people who have _not,_ than there are those who _have._ Those _prisoners with_ the money and education control those _without._ Their pain and misery, goes _unnoticed_ by the government. As with _any_ maximum-security prison, from the _outside_ there is _no way to tell, what_ is happening _inside._

Recently, a 27-year old Black man was brought to me at the Jail. He was a quadriplegic. He _lived,_ in a specially-designed wheelchair that doubled as his bed. Although his commitment papers stated that he was 27, his _emaciated and lifeless body, was that of a 10-year old child._ His body wastes went into a _bag,_ attached to him. His mouth moved his wheelchair-bed, through a long _tube,_ which came up to his chin. He had arrived from court, _before_ the normal flow of returning prisoners, and *new* intakes for the day. I was dumbfounded.

What kind of *crime* <u>could</u> this man violate, to have him <u>here</u> at my strip-search table? When I asked him, he quietly and haltingly replied around his tube, "I was arrested for possession of marijuana." As he was arrested on Saturday, he had spent the week-end in Central cellblock, as there is no court on Sundays. Today, at his arraignment at court where he pleaded guilty, the judge sentenced this man to *10-days in jail for possession of <u>marijuana</u>*. I discovered later, that this was his *first offense*. When I asked him what *race* the arresting officer was, he answered "Black." I then asked him, what about the judge? He replied, "Black."

I had nothing more, to say. Although I <u>refused</u> to lift him onto the clothes-examination table, and physically *strip* him. *That, I <u>could not</u> do.* Other correctional staff, more dedicated to their jobs, did this. I excused myself from the room, as I didn't want anyone working with me, to see my angry tears. Several days later, I learned that this man *died while in our custody.* I don't *know* if he died as a *result* of being incarcerated at the C.T.F.? What I *do* know is that he *died, incarcerated for a minor offense, <u>away</u> from his <u>family</u> that <u>loved</u> him.* America, <u>read</u> the "Declaration of Independence."

"We hold these truths to be self-evident, that all Men are created equal, that they are endowed by their Creator with certain unalienable Rights,

that among these are Life, Liberty, and the Pursuit of Happiness–That to secure these Rights, Governments are instituted among Men, deriving their just Powers from the Consent of the Governed, that whenever any Form of Government becomes destructive of these Ends, it is the Right of the People to alter or to abolish it, and to institute new Government, laying it's Foundation on such Principles, and organizing its Powers in such Form, as to them shall seem most likely to effect their Safety and Happiness. Prudence, indeed, will dictate that Governments long established should not be changed for light and transient Causes; and accordingly all Experience hath shewn, that Mankind are more disposed to suffer, while Evils are sufferable, than to right themselves by abolishing the Forms, to which they are accustomed...."

WHAT COMES AROUND, GOES AROUND

The three circles of long-term confinement. The 'first' circle is the prison itself. The 'second' circle, are the officers, and their authority and rules. The 'third' circle, are those prisoners who *control* other prisoners *inside* of the last circle. In the District of Columbia, and *wherever* there are substantial numbers of Blacks, the three 'circles' of prison are always in effect. Only since Black people have been allowed to integrate into White society, and left their 'slave quarters,' has this anomaly changed. Now, the *'trustees'* are wholly in-charge.

When 'freed' from the various plantations in 1865, segregation forced us into Black 'prison camps.' There, the *same institutional behaviors* (although relaxed by our "extended parole") began to take form. The *only* thing that changed was the size of the plantation.

Blacks were forced to stay together, and work was cheap and plentiful. We could come and go as we pleased on "our side of town," but had to be wary on "Master's" part of the plantation. The 'slave catchers' (now uniformed) patrolled the borders, and kept a watchful eye out for 'troublemakers and runaways.'

Can anyone reading this understand how *tragic* this intentional *manipulation* of an abused people has been? After being cruelly imprisoned and used for generations, denied the natural rights and liberties due all human beings, this group of *domesticated* Black people were hoaxed *again*. Their 'ownership' was *transferred to the federal government*, and their 'custody' became *transparent*. Yet they were in no better condition than they were before. Still 'slaves,' and still 'owned.' During our hundreds of years of captivity, our 'institutionalization' required *the erasure of any memory of what 'self-rule' or 'sovereignty' meant.*

Absolutely gone from our memory, is the truth that what "makes *a people*" are *their own constitution and laws*. We call ourselves "African-American." We are neither. We say that we are "one people." We are not. We live a fantasy, built on generations of cruelty and lies. It is time to awaken to the truth. It is time to protect ourselves, and to throw off the shackles on our minds. Black children are dying. Black communities are war-zones. And the only ones that can stop this march into genocide are "us." But we must do this as a *united people*, under the law. *'We' must make our own laws.*

When will *all* of us, recognize this as truth? Black people, shake off the 'drug' of 'generational institutionalization,' and start the discussions needed to awaken others. White people, those of you who read this and were ignorantly unaware of the truth revealed to you here until now, take a stand for the truth. Black people must be free to choose their own destiny. *We have never been given a choice*. We have never been offered *treatment* for the generations of brainwashing. "We" *canno*t *be a people* without *the right to choose to be a people*. We must be given that right, or eventually, we will *force* that right. *When* will it *happen*?

If America doesn't act now, the answer will be, when we get "caught-up." Are you *familiar* with the expression? It means someone who becomes a *victim* of the *circumstances* around him. For example, the music in the disco is loud and exciting. Many people are dancing all around, and having fun. The average person walking into this fun scene can get 'caught up,' in the moment. He starts nodding his head to the beat of the music, and his mood livens. The next thing you know, the guy starts dancing and smiling. He is having fun, and has *just* become 'caught up' in the moment.

The *majority* of Black people in America live on or below the levels of poverty. They run a gauntlet of fear and possible violence every day, just to survive. Their anger and frustration with the 'system,' grows and grows. One day, without warning, *something* is going to *break*. Maybe it will be the violent murder by some crazed White man, of a beloved Black 'leader.' Maybe it will be the *one* Black child, shot dead in the ghetto, that was *one too many*. Maybe, it will come as a result of some Black-Alpha male, saying to the masses over and over again, "enough is enough."

In whatever form the break comes, a *portion* of Black America *will* erupt. And, like hot molten lava running down the sides of a volcano, it will burn everything in its path. The number of disenfranchised Blacks, who have nothing to lose, *far outnumbers those Blacks who do*. What will you do, America? Will you *spare* your Black '*trustees*,' your *lash*? Will you *trust them*, to help you *control the Black mob*? No. You will not. Did you trust Japanese-Americans, after the attack on Pearl Harbor? No. Did you trust Muslim-Americans, after the September 11th bombings? No.

The *racism* of the *silent majority* is alive and well, and *hiding* behind the Constitution of the United States. If poor Blacks vent their anger on America, what will *America's* response be, towards *all Black people*? Whether you are *for*, or *against*? You already know. It doesn't matter, does it? The sick acceptance on *both sides*, of a color-caste mentality of 'one united Black people,' will cause America to react against *all Black-skinned people*. You who are the '*trustees*,' are you ready? When 'Marshall Law' is declared, will it take you by complete surprise?

If it *does*, then you *deserve* to be *surprised*. If you had *remained* in the neighborhoods (now ghettoes), that you originally *came from,* you would have *known* that your 'people' are *ready* to blow. 'Black' America, do you *realize* how *dependent you really are,* on the largess of White America? In a 'state of emergency,' how would *you* survive, if White people *temporarily cut-off their support?* Do any of you have:

- Two-weeks supply of clean water for drinking, cooking, and bathing?
- One month's supply of food in your home, that doesn't need refrigeration?
- Emergency cash on hand, when the banks close?
- A back-up generator and candles, when the electricity is shut-off?
- An emergency first-aid kit and necessary medications?
- Mobile communications when the telephone lines go down?
- Reliable transportation and gasoline, when the stations close?
- Are your Life and Property insurances paid?

Will White-owned companies, reimburse you for Black-"backlash?" Prepare yourselves now. After the last fiery reactions to what Blacks perceived as injustice, 'White' America has learned a terrible lesson. It will *not* be so easily caught unawares, again. Remember Rodney King? I was one of *thousands* of police officers, recalled to duty that night. The night *thousands* of Black people, took to the streets of the cities of America, angry about the beating, and the verdicts. Fortunately, unlike the 'King' before him, *he* didn't *die.* If he *had,* Black folk would have been 'caught up.'

After the *certain* civil unrest and violence of that night, we would have *all* suffered America's wrath, because of our Black skin. After so many years of 'generational-institutionalization,' we are now 'conditioned.' We have so *many* generations *accepting as a fact,* that a 'White'-skinned man could <u>own</u> a 'Black'-skinned man, that levels of superiority and inferiority are *deeply* ingrained into our minds. Do you *see* how *many* Black youth are standing-by, *waiting* for something like this to happen? How many are on the streets, without jobs? They are angry and frustrated.

Have you *talked to them?* Do you *listen to their music?* Do *any* of you educated Black *middle and upper middle-class, know how they feel?* You should, if only to prepare yourselves. *Their* savagery and uncontrollable anger *will* have a *lasting effect* on how America *treats <u>you</u>* after the lights come back on. As always, America will push *you out in front,* to calm and soothe the masses. It has worked in the *past,* and they will assume, that it will work *again.* Suppose it *doesn't?* What will *you* do? In *every* nation of the world, the poor and disenfranchised have eventually revolted. Imagine the anger of a people "kept in a bottle" for five-hundred years!

'America' needs to stop worrying about the

problems of the *world,* and concentrate on the problems within its *own* borders. Billions of dollars spent for space exploration. Billions of dollars spent for war. Billions of dollars 'invested' in foreign aid. Billions of dollars spent to bail-out various American industries. Yet, to *stop* the problems that plague 'Black' people in America, nothing. I envision you having meetings, summits, and conferences, to *discuss* the 'issues.' And *who* will 'representing' the masses of poor Black people *at* these meetings? Elitist Blacks, who wouldn't have a *clue,* as to <u>*what*</u> *disenfranchised* Black people are feeling today. Why, are *they* considered the 'leaders' of poor Black people? The standards of 'colonialism' *never* change. After 'conquering' an African people, historically, Europeans installed their *own* puppet regimes in African nations. Specially - groomed Blacks, who *they* felt, 'were doing what was *best* for <u>*those people.'*</u> These 'puppet-leaders,' helped their 'masters,' to *severely exploit* their *own people.* The same 'colonial' mentality, survives in America, today. This is your final warning, America. *Let my people go,* before it is too late.

A DECLARATION OF INDEPENDENCE

In my booklet of "The U.S. Constitution-and fascinating facts about it," is a copy of the "Declaration of Independence." Earlier, I quoted from it. *This,* is how it *begins.*

"Action of Second Continental Congress, July 4, 1776

The unanimous Declaration of the thirteen United States of America

WHEN in the course of human Events, it becomes necessary for one People to dissolve the Political Bands which have connected them with another, and to assume among the Powers of the Earth, the separate and equal Station to which the Laws of Nature and of Nature's God entitle them, a decent Respect to the Opinions of Mankind requires that they should declare the causes which impel them to the Separation..."

It is 7:45 a.m. I am helping the U.S. Marshals Service, load-up over one-hundred Black male prisoners onto their buses. These men are going to Superior and U.S. District Court, here in Washington, D.C. Each week-day morning, the *same* drama is played-out *over* and *over again*. The men strip naked, and go through a cursory visual *inspection* of their genitals and spread buttocks. Each of them stands in front of the *inspection table*, one at a time. After they dress, the Marshals signal that it's time to load them up.

The men are called by name and D.C. number. Each man is then *handcuffed* and *shackled* at the waist and ankles. When they are finished, each 'load' is put in a large enclosed *cage*, awaiting their turn to go to the buses. Do you remember me telling you before, that although both jails held over three-thousand men that day, only approximately *100* were White? Here, is where you *really* see the disparity of race. Here, is where the image of one-hundred Black men *chained and shackled*, is a *vivid reminder of the horrors of the slave market*.

To be a Black Correctional Officer, and <u>witness</u> this *extraordinary sight*, is like being *transported <u>back</u> two-hundred years ago*. I feel a haunting sadness. I *know* what you are thinking. "These men committed some *crime*, so they *deserve* to be treated this way!" Not so. There is 'due process.' That means *that a man or woman charged with a crime, is <u>presumed innocent</u> until <u>proven</u> guilty, by a court of law*. So *until* such time as they *are* found 'guilty' by a *judge or jury*, what *I* see each morning, are over *one-hundred shackled Black men who may be innocent.* Many are the *same* men that I see on the *outside* of the Jail when I go home.

There are many *'poor' people,* who break the law, so that they can put food on their tables. They make no excuses, or ask for anyone's pardon. They live a day-by-day existence, hand to mouth. These millions, no longer hope that their lives will be better. And it is *this* core of resignation that I rebel against. These Black people *can* be helped. Poverty and ignorance *can* be eliminated. There is *no problem* plaguing the Black community that *cannot* be *resolved* by a concerted effort on the part of *all* of the people. How can we overcome the obstacles?

There are examples, all *around us.* Many Black people in America do not *know* the history of the *other* stolen Africans. Where did they go? What happened to them? The 'middle-passage' that brought the tens of millions of different Africans to the 'New World,' *didn't bring all of us to North America!* The *majority* of Africans went to the *south* of this country. Over the years, unlike those that came *here,* they *revolted* against their colonial masters. Destroyed what had *been,* and created *new* foundations which *included them all, as one people.*

Cuba, Dominican Republic, Haiti, Jamaica, Guatemala, Barbados, Costa Rica, French Guiana, Trinidad and Tobago, Guyana, Panama, Brazil, Honduras, etc. Many of them, then mixed with the native populations, and became *exactly* what the majority of descendants of Africans in *America* are today. We are largely a mixed-blooded people of African, Native-American, and European descent. But we have a very different 'history' from our ancestors who were taken to these other countries. Once freed by rebellion, revolution, or through voluntary relinquishing of power, their country's 'constitution,' was *also* changed.

Your *cousins* became an *integral* part of *each* of their nations. They were no longer just a *'Black' part* of their nations, afforded an 'amnesty.' *All* of the people became *one*. They *do not refer to themselves, or separate themselves, by color*. They are "Cubans." They are "Jamaicans." They are "Dominicans." They are "Haitians," etc., etc. Their economic standards of living may be much lower than North America's, but they live as *one people*. What does it mean to the 'Black' American individual, to have all of the money in the world, and *be alone? That is our reality*.

The United States *prohibited* me from legally enjoining my *own* race, after 1865. While we were confused from incarceration, and shocked with our 'parole,' we failed to recognize that we needed to create a *constitutional avenue* to becoming legitimately *one people*. This comes with the *right* to elect leadership, the *right* to live in 'peace and tranquility' amongst my *own*, and the *right* to self-defense of my person and property. The knowledge, that as *one people, we* can determine our path *together*.

This dream is recognized by *every other nation, containing the lost children of Africa.* Instead of embracing these *other* nationalities of African descent and *learning* from them, *in our loneliness we seek to cover them with our 'Blackness.'* I have asked many of these non-Americans, why *they* haven't said anything to *us,* when they come here and see the way we treat each other? A grown man can learn from a child, if he listens. Doesn't *everyone* in the 'Black Diaspora' *who has sovereignty,* see *immediately* the solution to Black America's problem? That our 'indoctrination' into imprisonment, blinded us to what makes a 'people?'

That the White man taught us that 'we' are one people because we are all Black, and that we accepted this lie, and continue to perpetrate it? No, they *don't* see us for the confused and separated group we are. The issue of *their* sovereignty, versus our *lack* of sovereignty, is *forgotten once they arrive amongst us!* They don't *recognize* that Blacks in America are *still living within* the bondage of colonialism that *they* have fought off! They *assume* our 'citizenship,' was secured by the same means that *they* restructured *theirs.* All of them are so blinded by our wealth, and education, that even *they* don't see the truth.

If 'we' are really one 'people,' then tell me *who* is in 'charge' of "African-Americans?" *Everyone* says "no one is *in charge of me*, but *me*." In that case, we *must* recognize that we are *not a 'people.'* We are only a *'group'* of people, *owing allegiance to none. That* is *dangerous* to the group itself. We ignorantly create our own chaos and anarchy. I *refuse* to be labeled a 'color,' as part of my nationality. I *need* to bond with those who suffer *with* me, but I *cannot*, because the current *reasons for* our bonding are *insubstantial*.

We bond, because we share the same darkened *skin*-color. We bond, because we share the same religion. We bond, because we share the same educational and economical *assimilation* skills. We bond, because we *like* each other. We bond, because we share the same *political* views. 'African-Americans' live within a paradox. We *are* a people, but we have no *control* over the actions of our group. Those *individuals* among us that have successfully assimilated, *know* the answers to the masses misery, but have no <u>power</u> to create change for the *whole*.

We are a 'nation' *separated*, by our own ignorance. To those who have a *reason* for being, life is *precious*. My 'Black-skinned' people, *have* no *reason* for '*being*' *except slavery*, and *that* is the reason for their anger. That is the *real* reason for their killing. To Black men in America, I pose two questions? These are the same tow questions which I ask *all* men from *other* nations, which 'restructured' their constitutions. "Would you give your *life*, for your Mother and Father?" Their answer is of course, "yes." I *then* ask them "would you give your *life*, for your *country?*" *All of them, without hesitation answer, "<u>Yes</u>, I <u>would</u>."*

How did *you* answer these two questions, in *your* heart? So *many* 'Black' men have confessed that the *only* reason *they* joined the military of the United

States, was because it offered a way-off of the streets. Or, they were "drafted," and couldn't face a *criminal conviction*. All received a 'check,' three-meals a day, clothing, education, and a chance to see the world. *That's* what *many* have stated was *their* reason for joining this nation's armed forces. When talking to *me, <u>none</u>* of their reasons for military service had to do with "love of country."

Are you Black *Americans, or* did *America, make you 'Black?'* It's time to tell the truth, don't you think?

"All that is necessary for the forces of evil to win in the world is for enough good men to do nothing." – Edmund Burke (1729-97), Irish-born British politician, writer.

THE ANSWER TO WHY?

I finally understand what happened, to make African-Americans act the way that they do individually and collectively. In order to grasp the significance of my ending, you have to examine several *different* dynamics affecting this group over so long a period of time. Kidnaping, imprisonment for hundreds of years, torture, brainwashing, cultural substitution, false racial-identification, and long-term institutionalized-prisoner behavior, created this *unique* "tribe" of 40-million people. I say unique, because *never before* in the history of the world, has a prisoner-group suffered such a transformation and evolution.

Everyone sees what their mind and training says are a "people." They see a "Black" people, who are miraculously connected by the color of their skins alone. Much like the Africans who first saw groups of Whites living together, may have erroneously thought that they were "of the same tribe," but were not. The American lie of bonding a group of people together, and wholly considering them to be "one people," came from the brutality of slavery. Whites, then and now, considered all of us "one Negro people" without consideration of our original sovereign differences.

The conditions of our shared oppression, as well as the institutionalized behaviors taught us during our captivity, made us *forget* that we were *not* "the same people." That in order to become a "people," *laws must be created with the consent of the majority*, to *create* this unity. Disrespected as human beings and thrown into forced labor as prisoners, the disrespect *continues to this day*, by the failure of *both sides* to understand that *like skin-color* is not enough to create a "people" or to guarantee safety amongst this "same skin-color group." Whites arrogantly *refuse to recognize this fact*, and *Blacks have forgotten this fact* through long-term imprisonment.

There were no walls to our prison. It was this foreign land and the color of our skins that made and identified us as a prisoner-group. Excluding Black people from the benefits of this society because of the color of our skins, *kept the prisoner group (and the lie) together*, long after the physical imprisonment ended. The institutionalized behavior was set, after so long a period of indoctrination. Whites had become "White people," and Blacks had become "Black people." But had they really? Whites realized after 283-years together (1493-1776), that the mutual coloring of their skins *would not be enough* to change their instinctive hatred for each other's nationality.

French would hate English, English would hate German, German would hate Dutch, and on and on. So they guaranteed peace between themselves, and created "E Pluribus Unum" (out of many, one) by creation of a new *constitution*. One that would ensure equal rights for each of the different parts, now blended into one. *This* is the way all of the free "people" of the world become a "people." It is *not* how Blacks in America became "one." Whites *made* us "one people," by hatred and segregation. Whites *made* us "one" by their racist mentality that *all* Black people come from some mysterious Black country named "Africa."

What would have happened to the massive group of white-skinned people who inhabit this country today, if their ancestors had *not* been wise enough to join together their separate parts into a constitutionally-united whole? Which single incident would have sparked war between them, based upon their different ancestral heritages? Like it did in their mother countries? The original Europeans who lived together from 1493 until 1776 without a "constitution," argued amongst and killed each other with no thought of their mutual skin color. Now that you see the truth in my words, *re*-examine Blacks in America.

Many African tribes were decimated to create the

beginnings of our "race" in North America. Over hundreds of years, all of these *different tribal prisoners* were forcibly "bred" and brainwashed into *one new group*. These *different tribes of people* (that is the key to this puzzle) were forcibly taken from their homelands, and brought to this country as labor. As prisoners, they suffered 'institutionalization,' during their *generations-long* incarceration. In the period between the *first*-generation's anger and confusion, and the *second*-generation's *breaking*, two words in our spoken language were *substituted* for two others.

"*Imprisonment*" and "*prisoner,*" have been surreptitiously replaced, by "*slavery*" and "*slave.*" In Webster's Dictionary, "imprisonment" is defined as, "*to restrain, limit, or confine as if in a prison.*" And the word "prisoner," is defined as, "*one kept in custody, captivity, or a condition of forcible restraint...*" As *Americans*, we know from experience or history, what "imprisonment" is. And most importantly, we know that there are *reasons* for a person to be imprisoned. According to America's system of laws, a person may be imprisoned if convicted of a crime. Once the sentence is served, the prisoner is released.

Our ancestors *committed no crime* against the colonists, who became "Americans," yet they became "prisoners" nonetheless. In a sense, they became prisoners of war. On the continent of Africa, wars were waged. Whole tribes and villages were attacked by their enemies. After conquest, these *enemy* tribes were 'sold' to Europeans, who transported these tribes of people to faraway lands as a perverse 'commerce.' These *prisoners* of long forgotten African wars, had their custody *transferred,* to *citizens* of different nations of *Europe*. In *our* case, these 'colonists,' *settled* our ancestors here. Our ancestors were **prisoners**, <u>*not*</u> *'slaves.'*

The *anger* of *my* first ancestor, who was dragged-off of that long-ago ship, is a vivid and recurring nightmare in my soul. He or she was confused, beaten, and shackled. He or she suffered *untold horrors*, confined in the belly of a ship, on a journey to an unknown land. He or she realized with despair, that each mile at sea was taking him or her farther away from home and freedom. At the end of this journey, my ancestor had to suffer the indignity and shame of a 'slave-market.' In my mind, I can picture the screaming heartache of seeing wife and children, torn from you forever. To be 'sold' in lots to the highest White-skinned bidder.

Prisoners, universally, are *made* to submit to their imprisonment. Outnumbered, shackled and restrained, *what could my ancestor do?* Self-preservation is the first rule of nature. These horribly abused prisoners, survived. Through sheer strength of will, they survived. What of the barbaric and cold-blooded White-skinned men who imprisoned them? They did not look upon my ancestor, *as a prisoner of war.* They did not view them as men and women, who *although prisoners*, were *due* dignity and respect. No. These *barbarians* of white-skin color believed in their hearts and minds, that my ancestor was a savage beast, and now *property*.

They truly believed the black color of his skin, made him *sub*-human. They believed that *all* black-skinned people were sub-human, and could be *bought and sold like the cattle in their fields*. A sick European 'colonist' transferred my ancestor's condition of *imprisonment* as a *man or woman,* to that of the 'holding of chattel.' 'Prisoner,' *became 'slave,'* and *'imprisonment' became 'slavery.'* When you torture and brainwash your prisoners, to make *them* believe in *your* sickness, that brainwashing does *not* become *truth. It only replaces the truth with your lie.* After so many generations, the lie becomes reality, and the truth is forgotten by conditioning.

Three-hundred years of *reinforced* brainwashing *ingrains* and *solidifies* that conditioning. The truth is that a man can *only* hold another man *a prisoner.* He *cannot <u>own</u> another human being.* Not then, or now. He can only *hold* that man or woman, against his or her will. They are still *human beings.* To think otherwise, is *in*-human. That's what these colonists were, and *that's* what the legally-consolidated *'Americans,'* inherited. Americans inherited 'in-humanity' in form and deed, to even *consider* the imprisonment of another human being for their labor, a 'just cause.' Without dialogue on this issue, hostility festers and burns within this prisoner-group.

What *crime*, did my ancestor commit, against these 'colonial-European' men? To make them *incarcerate my family for over three-hundred years?* What caused them to take their humanity away, and *replace* it, with the mentality of a domesticated animal? *All* colonists, whether 'slave-holder' or *not, allowed* this treachery. All, whether they believed in 'slavery' or not, *also believed* that *my* ancestors were *inferior to White-skinned people.* Europeans *began* this identification of 'Black-skin,' and 'White-skin.' *Superiority* and *inferiority* became conditions of the prisoner's learned 'institutionalized behavior.'

We were in-bred, for more 'stock.' Over generations we became *many* of *one*-blood, from *the groups* of *separate and sovereign tribes and nations.* Yet, through the conditions of our *incarceration,* we *remained strangers* to each other. *This foolishness must end.* No 'people' can live together, without creating their own laws. *No* 'people,' can plot their destiny *together, without lawful unification. No* 'people,' are a *'people,'* because of the *color* of their *skin.* What was set in motion by the intentional brainwashing of this massive group in the past, *perpetually* affects all of us 'Black' and 'White,' in the present. There is no other explanation.

What was done to us was *horribly wrong. Everyone* is taken *to the point of tears,* when the *horrors of that time* are explained to them. But *none of us* can shake ourselves *out of the ignorance taught to our ancestors!* If we *truly believe* that no man has the *right* to *own* another human being, then *why* do we all *acknowledge and continue to use a very effective weapon of the 'institutionalization' process?* Why don't we *recognize that we were not 'slaves?'* To *continue* this lie by even *uttering* this word, *is to acknowledge that lie as a fact*, and *belittles our righteous claims for justice.* **I am not a descendant of 'slaves!'** *No one 'owned' my ancestors!*

Continued use of this word 'slave,' also *subconsciously denigrates or emboldens the speaker*, depending upon his or her race. When a White man hears the word 'slave,' he unconsciously thinks of 'Negro property,' and 'superiority.' When a Black man hears the word 'slave,' he unconsciously thinks 'Master' and 'inferiority.' It is the 'training' that is still in effect, when you think like a barbarian thinks. Stop using the word 'slave.' The need for sovereignty is paramount to our survival in America. Whites knew this in 1776. If it were not an important part of the unification process, *why did they go to such lengths to ensure its success amongst themselves?*

And how then, do you explain the fact that *none* of *them* understands that *we* need *unification* *ourselves, to stop our killing?* That *we* need the *same* constitutional sovereignty they made for themselves, to be whole as a "people." This is such a simple solution. A 'solution' *their* ancestors came up with *themselves, in 1776.* When *you* have done this for *yourselves,* and *ignore* these same rights and benefits for *your abused prisoners,* are you *ignorant* or *stupid?* 'Black' people do not *recognize* the need, because these *basic truths* have been washed-*out* of us, *over these over 300-years of 'ownership.'* Washed-out of us due to 'generational-institutionalization.'

This massive group of prisoners had been denied free-will for so long, that the thought of *legally-*

combining the separated tribal parts that had been made into a "new whole" over the centuries, *never occurred to them after emancipation*. It is a continuation of our misery when Black and mulatto people *created from the incubation of generations of imprisonment*, remain a second-class group *trapped* within a constitutionally-created white majority. We are spitefully denied constitutional binding to create a lawful and unified people, who can then create laws for their own protection. Why can't we see this fact for ourselves?

It is because after the death of the first-generation, *'institutionalization' of all of the generations of their descendants,* became a certainty. A certainty, that born into captivity, *none of the children* would *remember* what freedom *ever was.* A certainty that once labeled a falsely united 'black' group, none of the children would remember that they were *not "one people."* The slave-markets destroyed their families and tribes. Their identities were lost. They were each alone, imprisoned within the greater White society. America never gave closure to its gross crime against these people. ***It simply walked away from the whole misadventure.***

Emancipation was given, and nothing else. Something that *existed only in their minds* was 'abolished' (transferred). After so many generations of cruel captivity, the now-formed 'black people,' tried to make the best of their woeful lives. Jim Crow and segregation pursued them for over 100-years. Finally, *overt* segregation ended, but the die had been cast.

These strangers to each other, black-skinned prisoners, found themselves *believing* the lie taught them. The lie whispered in their ear, that because they were 'black,' they were one people. The lie told them that as a "people," they could from 1865 on responsibly control one another without law.

The truth that *this is a lie* has been revealing itself since 'integration.' We were then, and are now, all different from each other. With no formal law to bind us and to guide us, we are destroying each other, with no way to stop it. The behavior of my entire "race" in America *duplicates the behavior of long-term prisoners inside of a prison.* We are the only 'people' in the world, *formed* by the conditions of our imprisonment, and by our mutual skin-color. Ironic, that as one of America's 'protected' class of people *we share no 'protections' from each other.* We *are* free. Free to wantonly kill each other, with no way for "us" to stop it.

The constitutionally-united group that captured us then, *still* controls us today with *their* laws. *We* never created laws, for ourselves. *This* paradox is what is destroying us. The conditions of our captivity, *created* the sickness that survives generationally, in all of us. We are identified as ex-*slaves* (property) by the color of our skin, amongst ourselves and by all others around us. As long as racism survives in America, we are doomed to be participating victims. This was done *to* us, and we *continue* to do this, *to* each other. As a result, we attack and kill each other, because that is the way of life for *all* prisoners sharing nothing but their imprisonment together.

Our "race" was *intentionally* created, by the forced mixing of our individual sovereign blood. But *what is our future here together* without unification by law? If we do not stop our own blind advance, we *will* continue to suffer here, separated. The *only* reason you *continue* to call me 'Black,' is because my *master* called me 'Black.' The *only* reason you *continue* to call me 'nigger,' is because my *master* called me 'nigger.' The *only* reason you continue to call me 'brother,' is because our *master*, <u>*whipped*</u> us into one 'family.' These things are *not* who I am, they are what I was *made* to be, to *break* me. We should not *trust* what we have *no control over*. Without our *own* sovereignty, and constitutional laws <u>*that carry penalties amongst ourselves*</u>, we die. We *want* to be accepted by 'America,' but *first* we must be accepted by each *other*. The sad truth for many of us is that all we *have* <u>*is*</u> the color of our skins. The *reason* for our persecution and segregation has become the *comfort* in our lives. Our proud and singular 'blackness' created from a European's lie, is now our strength. Unfortunately, because we refuse to recognize the truth of our own sickness, we innocently cling to our own killers and murderers. This group of freed ex-'slaves,' is beset with internal strife and self-inflicted violence.

We are self-destructive, and live without purpose other than survival. There is *presently* no *legal* way for the 'group' to *control* its *own* actions, so when 'America's' police are *not* watching, the conditions of *our learned imprisonment* rule. By design, the Black family structure is slowly disintegrating. Families are becoming more and more dysfunctional. Black women, without the strength and guidance of the Black man, are *raising and harboring the murderers of our race.* The real truth is now apparent. Our community's 'unity' *without* segregation to *enforce* our 'togetherness,' *is* and *always will be* a dream.

What say you, America? *Is there a way* to allow Black people to become *sovereign, without seceding from your 'Constitution?* Then *together,* deciding *ourselves,* whether to become 'Americans' *as a sovereign people?* That way, we *break* the spell of being a 'color' of separated people under it, as we are now. White folk, instead of 'sharing' *your sovereignty,* can we both share our own, *together? Like you do with the Native-American?* It can be done, and one day, it will be done. Whites lived together in this country from 1493 until 1776 without an ideal of constitutionality. *We* have only been free to choose, since 1865. We have time to decide our fate.

I closed my notebook, satisfied that I had finished my quest. Unification would bring peace, but with so many calls for unity for the wrong reasons, the *reality of our dis-unity* has become obscured. The poor woman who lost her son to street violence, demanded to know "Why?" I investigated the question, pieced together the evidence, clues, eyewitness statements, and back-tracked to a possible motive. In short, I have come to an answer based upon *my* research and analysis. I have discovered that these brown and black-skinned people, my people, are *confused and separated* from the effects of over three-hundred years of brainwashing and de-humanizing programming.

That 5,000,000 black and brown-skinned prisoners from *many* different tribes, created the largest single African "tribe" in existence today. *40,000,000 people of the same blood*, the same trapped condition of existence, and the same destiny. They are still huddling together for warmth and security, taught by their "*masters*" to stay together, but without constitutional laws to control their massive "race." There was just *one* more thing that I *had* to do. I went back to that poor woman's home that I walked out of so many years ago. I wanted to talk to her about what I had discovered. Share with her the twists and turns of my quest.

In some small way, bring her some comfort in the knowledge that a great sickness claimed her son. But she was gone, and a new family lived where she had been. All I wanted was to let her know *how much* her anguished question *meant* to me, those long years ago. I wanted to bring some closure to the haunting question she presented to me. I had a vague idea of what I might have said to her. I *would* have said "sister, your son was killed *because he believed that being 'Black' was enough for him to survive on the streets of 'Black' America.*

He was killed because he was taught that the color of his skin, gave him *automatic protection* amongst those whose *skin*-color was the same as his. *All of us, within Black America, <u>taught him</u>* this. *We were wrong*, and the lie cost him his life. In our hearts, we are still the savage prisoners that we were forced to become, by the conditions of our imprisonment. A prison does *not* have to have walls and bars, to be a prison. And imprisonment does not always end with that prisoner's death. We are *all* to blame. It's taken me years to 'close this case.' Here is my 'report,' of the *reasons* 'Black' men *kill* 'Black' men. *Here* is the *answer*, to your question of Why?"

REFERENCES

Cover (And all references thereof): "The United States Constitution and Fascinating Facts About It" copyrighted 1993, by Oak Hill Publishing Company written or compiled by Robert F. Tedeshi, Jr.

Chapters 2,3, 7, 13: "Dark Faces, Hard Times" copyrighted 2002, by Allan E. Lucas, Jr., Washington, D.C.

Chapter 3: "The District of Columbia Emancipation Act" An Act approved by the Congress, April 16, 1862 U.S. National Archives and Records Administration

Chapter 4: "The Emancipation Proclamation" Abraham Lincoln, January 1, 1863

Chapter 4: an excellent interpretation, given by Mr. Lerone Bennett, Jr., in his article in Ebony Magazine, February 2000 copyrighted. Also, read his book, "Forced into Glory: Abraham Lincoln's White Dream," published by Johnson Publishing Company, copyrighted 1999.

Chapter 6: first reference of *Two America's, Black and White*, by the "Kerner Commission Report" on the state of American race relations, published in 1968. Available for reading at the Martin Luther King, Jr. Library, Washington, D.C.

Chapter 9: for additional information on Black Nationalism, read "The Rediscovery of Black Nationalism" by Theodore Draper, copyrighted and published by Viking Press, 1970.

Chapter 12: American racism as an ingrained institution. Read "Anyplace But Here" by Arna Bontemps and Jack Conroy, New York: published by Hill and Wang, 1966

Chapter 13: Metropolitan Police Department, Office of Public Information: 300 Indiana Avenue, N.W. Wash. D.C. 20001; District of Columbia Superior Court, Information Desk: 500 Indiana Avenue, N.W. Wash. D.C. 20001; Central Detention Facility, 1901 D Street, S.E., Washington, D.C. 20003

ABOUT THE AUTHOR

Allan E. Lucas, Jr., is one of five generations of native-Washingtonians. He attended D.C. Public Schools, graduating from Eastern High School. He attended Pepperdine University, U.D.C. Dave Clarke School of Law, and holds a Master's degree from the University of Phoenix, majoring in Criminal Justice and Security. He is married, a proud father and grandfather, and resides in the District of Columbia. Allan served his country as a military police officer with the United States Marine Corps during the Vietnam War.

Until his retirement, he continued to serve as a Deputy U.S. Marshal, an officer with the Metropolitan Police Department, and as an officer with the D.C. Department of Corrections. Today Allan lectures on the theory of "generational-institutionalization" as the cause, and constitutional sovereignty as the solution, to Black America's problems. His epiphany (generational-institutionalization) occurred while working as a corrections officer in the Lorton Reformatory. Read his compelling stories of life in Lorton prison, "Dark Faces-Hard Times."

"Black, by nature
Proud, by choice
Marine, by destiny
American, by slavery"
A.E. Lucas, Jr. (1995)

ABOUT THE BOOK

An investigative and political analysis of race-relations of African-Americans in the United States that began with a mother's anguished question. It explores the myth of slavery, and the reasons for the continuing frustration and anger in Blacks in America. The United States created this land of "colors," Black and White, with many questions. This book answers the question of "Why?" for both sides, and the reasons for the simmering frustration, confusion, and anger in the hearts of these adopted Americans. Read "A View from Street Level-The Answer to Why?" Go to www.viewfromstreetlevel.com and begin the journey to free your mind and your soul. Peace.

Made in the USA
Lexington, KY
25 November 2019